Above: Letters from Robert Wise to his mother, with Tammy Wise's eyeglasses
Previous page: At Frank Carvill's mother's home in Carlstadt, N.J.

LIFE

Last Letters Home

VOICES OF
AMERICANS FROM
THE BATTLEFIELDS
OF IRAQ

FOREWORD BY
SENATOR JOHN McCAIN

LIFE Books

Editor Robert Sullivan
Director of Photography Barbara Baker Burrows
Creative Director Carin Goldberg
Deputy Picture Editor Christina Lieberman
Photographer Dana Lixenberg
Senior Editor Malachy Duffy
Senior Designer Fon-Lin Nyeu
Writer-Reporters Hildegard Anderson (Chief), Adriana Gardella
Assistant Designer Anna Ostrovskaya
Copy Wendy Williams (Chief), Lesley Gaspar, Olga Han, Mimi McGrath
Production Michael Roseman (Manager), Leenda Bonilla (Assistant Manager), Yoshiko Canada
Picture Research Rachel Hendrick
Photo Assistant Joshua Colow
Contributing Editors Robert Andreas, JC Choi
Consulting Picture Editors Vivette Porges, Mimi Murphy (Rome), Tala Skari (Paris)

President Andrew Blau
Finance Director Varun Bedi
Operations Director Susan Popler-Roy
Creative Services Director Gail Chen
Business Development Manager Jeff Burak
Assistant to the President Sandy Green
Assistant Business Manager Karen Tortura
Assistant to the Operations Director Gretchen Weber

Editorial Operations Richard K. Prue (Director), Richard Shaffer (Manager), Brian Fellows, Raphael Joa, Stanley E. Moyse (Supervisors), Keith Aurelio, Gregg Baker, Charlotte Coco, Scott Dvorin, Kevin Hart, Rosalie Khan, Po Fung Ng, Barry Pribula, David Spatz, Vaune Trachtman, Sara Wasilausky, David Weiner

Special thanks to Anne-Michelle Gallero, Peter Giamanco, Carol Pittard, Jennifer Putrelo, Emily Rabin, David Shribman

Published by cds
President Gilbert Perlman
Senior Vice President, Client Services David Wilk
Special thanks to John Weber, Sensei Publications

The LIFE book *Last Letters Home* is based upon a documentary co-produced by HBO and *The New York Times* that bears the same title and that will have its premiere on Veterans Day, November 11, 2004. It is a film written and directed by Bill Couturié, produced by Bill Couturié and Anne Sandkuhler. The composer is Todd Boekelheide, the cinematographer Michael Chin, the editor Bill Weber and the associate producers are Ken Richards and Alexis Ercoli. For *The New York Times* the executive producer is Jane Bornemeier and the associate producers are Susan Ellingwood and Char Woods. For HBO the executive producers are John Hoffmann and Sheila Nevins.

LIFE gratefully acknowledges HBO and the support and commitment of Chris Albrecht, Chairman and CEO; Richard Plepler, Executive Vice President for Corporate Affairs; Sheila Nevins, Executive Producer and President of HBO Documentaries; and John Hoffman, Executive Producer. HBO also recognizes the special contributions of Michelle Boas, Bill Chase, Bill Imboden, Lana Iny, Brian Lutz, Jessica Manzi, Cindy Matero, Courteney Monroe, Peter Mozarsky, Jacqueline Norris, Richard Oren, Sharon Werner and Matt Young. HBO also extends a very special thanks to the families who welcomed us into their homes during this time of great difficulty.

Orders, inquiries and correspondence should be addressed to:
CDS
425 Madison Avenue
New York, NY 10017
(212) 223-2969 fax (212) 223-1504
www.lastlettershome.com

Please visit us, and sample past editions of LIFE, at www.LIFE.com.

ISBN: 1-593151-63-2

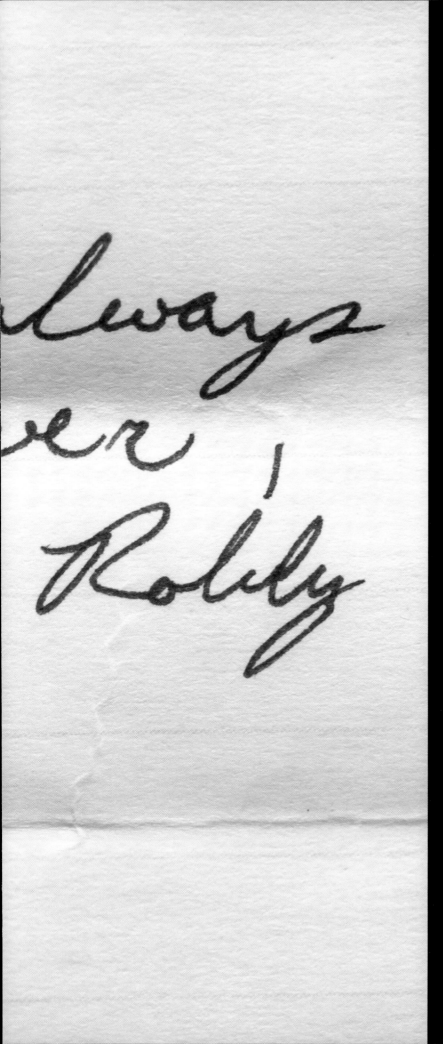

Left: The signature of Army Private Robert Frantz

About the Pictures in This Book

Dutch-born photographer Dana Lixenberg was a crucial part of LIFE's *Last Letters Home* project. Over the course of several weeks in August and September of 2004, she traveled from Florida to far northern Michigan, from Virginia to the island of Guam, making beautiful, honest, haunting images of 14 American families and their effects. Lixenberg's manner, which is both compassionate and professional, allowed her subjects to reveal themselves.

Lixenberg was brought to the *Last Letters Home* project by George Pitts, director of photography for the weekly LIFE. Lixenberg was aided in the logistics of her effort by photo assistant Stefanie Grätz and by Anne Sandkuhler, who has been working for much of the year on the HBO/*New York Times* documentary. Lixenberg's distinguished photographs for LIFE appear on pages 1, 20, 21, 26, 31, 39, 47, 53, 57, 61, 63 (right), 67, 71, 72, 77, 82, 87, 93, 99, 102, 107, 115, 119, 123, 128 and on the back cover.

LIFE would also like to thank the families themselves, who donated not only time and candor but many of the personal shots that document the younger years of their loved ones. This book is, in a very real way, their book.

Left: The signature of Army Private Robert Frantz

LIFE Books will donate partial proceeds from sales of this book to the Intrepid Fallen Heroes Fund. The fund provides unrestricted grants to the families of military personnel who have given their lives in the operations in Iraq and Afghanistan. The gifts, $11,000 to spouses and an additional $5,000 per child, are intended to help these families through any financial difficulties they may face, and to remind them that our nation appreciates the sacrifice they have made for us. The Intrepid Fallen Heroes Fund is supported entirely by donations. One hundred percent of contributions from the public for this effort go to support military families; the Fund's Board of Trustees underwrites all administrative costs. The Intrepid Fallen Heroes Fund is a 501(c)(3) organization and contributions are tax deductible under applicable laws.

To join this effort or for more information, visit www.fallenheroesfund.org or call 800-340-HERO.

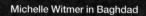
Michelle Witmer in Baghdad

A Lifeline

by Senator John McCain

Everybody would cheer. When I was onboard a ship, the greatest complaint was that the mail didn't get delivered regularly, or that we couldn't get our mail sent. We had a system called COD—Carrier Onboard Delivery—and when that plane touched down on the deck, everybody knew what it was, and they'd all cheer.

Letters, traveling in either direction during a war, are vital to morale—the most important item, I would say, when one is away from home and fighting a war. When you're writing a letter, you're back with your loved ones. You're *there* with them. And when you are reading what they've written, they're with you. It is comfort in an uncomfortable time.

When I was engaged in the Vietnam War I would write home often. Family was the highest priority, of course, but you also write to your friends. In peacetime, you tell them everything. When the war's on, you might hold back. Even when I was writing to my dad, it was never about military matters; it was personal stuff. That's what those letters are for—to connect.

The experience changed for me in prison. The North Vietnamese allowed us to write a five-line letter home, once a month. I received no mail. A lifeline had been cut. I couldn't express what I was feeling or thinking, and I didn't know for sure that my family understood my situation. I didn't receive a letter for four years. When you've lost something, you realize how much value it truly has. In 1968 when the Vietnamese offered me a chance to go home early, they gave me, during the interrogation, a letter from my wife that had been written long before, and that they'd been holding back—for whatever reason. Later, after my release, I learned that none of those short letters I had written had been sent. So all that time was spent in separation and fear.

A few years ago at a ceremony at the Library of Congress I read a letter aloud, one that you will read shortly in the essay that follows. It was written by a man who was on the *Forrestal* with me, and who died there. Robert Zwerlein wrote of being with his mates, singing "God Bless America" on a night not long before he died. It was incredibly moving, for me, to read that letter. And I didn't try to put a face with the name after all these years. A hundred and thirty-four men were killed on that ship, a number of them my friends. What I felt in reading one very personal, individual letter is that it spoke somehow for all involved in that war, at that time. Just as the letters in this book speak for those involved in this war, at this time.

I receive dozens of letters and e-mails each week from Iraq. They talk about courage, they talk about Iraq and Vietnam, they insist, most of them, that those in the field are convinced they are doing the right thing.

All of them are moving, as was Robert Zwerlein's letter. And all of them are important to read.

They allow us to connect.

John McCain, seen during his years at the Naval Academy in the 1950s (above with his father), is the son and grandson of Navy admirals. He was a prisoner of war from 1967 to 1973 in the notorious "Hanoi Hilton." When the North Vietnamese offered him early release in 1968, he refused, insisting that his stature should bring no privilege: He would wait for a general P.O.W. amnesty. McCain retired as a Navy Captain in 1981.

Letters Like No Others

The Messages From Iraq Are Part of a Heritage

They are not quite personal journals, but neither are they formal reports from the field. If they perchance contribute to the first draft of history, they are always more raw, more intimate, more candid and more introspective than "history." They are not simply letters home, but of course they *are* letters home. They are war letters.

They have been written since the ancient times, although in more distant wars they were far fewer, on account of illiteracy, meager resources (paper or writing tools) and the extreme unlikelihood that they would ever be delivered. A famous example: when the Greeks defeated the Persians at Marathon, the soldier Philippides was sent with the news to Athens. He ran nearly 30 miles, gave his report and, it is said, died on the spot. In today's wars, many communications are again aural, by phone or cell phone. Many others travel via e-mail.

The power inherent in a war letter, whatever its mode of transcription or delivery, is enormous. It is the creation of a person who is, by war's nature, imperiled. It is written by a man or woman who, for perhaps the first time in his or her life, is contemplating mortality, and is looking upon life, love, home and homeland in a dramatically new way.

In times gone by, as evinced by the tale of Philippides, the need to deliver news was certainly as important as the need to describe one's own plight. There were precious few professional war correspondents in 5th century B.C. Marathon or, indeed, Lexington, Mass., on April 19, 1775, when the "shot heard round the world" ignited the great American experiment. The following is from a letter by William Sutherland, a Britisher, a redcoat on the march.

"We still went on farther when three shot more were fired at us, which we did not return, and this is sacred truth as I hope for mercy . . . When we came up to the main body, which appeared to me to exceed four hundred in and about the village, who were drawn up in a plain opposite to the church, several officers called out, 'Throw down your arms and you shall come to no harm,' or words to that effect. Which, they refusing to do, instantaneously the gentlemen who were on horseback rode in amongst them, of which I was one, at which instant I heard Major Pitcairn's voice call out, 'Soldiers, don't fire; keep your ranks; form and surround them.' Instantly some of the villains, who got over the hedge, fired at us, which our men for the first time returned."

Sutherland was there—witness, combatant—but hardly ever delved into the personal because, in his day, circulating the account was paramount, and also seemly. The following is from the other side—the rebellious side—of the conflict, two months later, concerning the Battle of Bunker Hill. It is a report in two letters by Samuel Blachley Webb to his brother Joseph.*

"The Horrors and Devastations of War now begin to appear with us in Earnest," Webb began, and continued later: "After the Alarm, on our March down we met many of our worthy friends wounded sweltering in their Blood,—carried on the Shoulders of their fellow Soldiers—judge you what must be our feelings at this shocking Spectacle,—the orders were, *press on, press on,*—our Bretheren are suffering and will soon be cut of . . . but when we mounted the Summit, where the Engagement was,—good God how the Balls flew.—I freely Acknowledge I never had such a tremor come over me before . . . Opinions are various—and no returns yet made to the Council of Warr—but the best I can find out is about 120 of our Men kill'd and wounded, perhaps there may be double that number,—I cannot say . . . [W]e must retire before them & leave Cambridge to the Destruction of those merciless Dogs—but Heaven we trust will appear on our side,—and sure I am many thousands of Us must fall, before we flee from them."

Later: "Our Retreat on Saturday was Shameful & Scandalous, & owing to the Cowardice Misconduct & want of Regularity of the Province troops . . . One cluster would be sneaking down on their Bellies behind a Rock & others behind Hay cocks . . . [W]hen we came to rally & attempt to form again, we found it impossible, for they most all said they had no Officers to head them. In short the most of the Companies of this Province are commanded by a most Despicable set of Officers . . . Business here goes on very Dull—if any thing of importance heaves up it must go thro a long dispute in the Congress of near 200 Members & then thro a Committee of Safety & then a Committee of War & a Committee of Supplies & by that means they are forever doing Nothing."

Thus does Webb, a brigadier general in the Continental Army, conclude, in abject frustration, his account. He is quoted here at some length to illustrate how many characteristics of letters in this book were also present in the letters of our forefathers: the frank admission of fear, the harrowing description of confusion and misery, a casting of the conflict in religious terms, an abiding patriotism, a staunch commitment to never behave in a cowardly fashion and, lastly, a willingness to criticize the powers that be.

Note: Webb's letters have been condensed and blended, as letters will be throughout this book. LIFE's editors will endeavor to retain proper sense and context at all times. "Mistakes" of spelling or grammar will be retained unless they render a letter unintelligible.

In a letter to his father written in 1864, Confederate soldier J.R. Montgomery, whose blood stained the page, knew that his wound would soon prove mortal.

...ongive, me and Save
me, Give my love to
all my friends, my
strength fails me
my horse & my equip-
ments will be left
for you. Again a
long farewell to you
may we ever meet in heaven
Your Dying Son,
J.R. Montgomery

In recent years no one has done more reading of (and thinking about) war letters than Andrew Carroll of Washington, D.C., who, in 1998, founded the Legacy Project. His crusade to preserve the soldier's view from the battlefield has already led to the exemplary collection *War Letters: Extraordinary Correspondence from American Wars* and will, next year, yield a new book including letters from Iraq. In an interview, he spoke about the common aspects of war letters, then and now: "I had the opportunity to visit Baghdad after the invasion, albeit briefly, and both while I was there and afterward, as the troops started sharing their letters and e-mails with me, I kept thinking about how alike their messages are to those written generations and even centuries ago. Whether you go off with a musket or an M-16, the emotions of war just don't change. The language may be less formal these days. You may see cuss words appear with more frequency. But all of the same feelings—exhilaration, fear, determination, pride, courage, despair, homesickness—are there.

"It's interesting, the common perception is that Vietnam was the 'angry' war, while most others are considered 'just' and 'patriotic' wars. But while you can certainly find a great number of soldiers venting their frustration about being in Vietnam, you also find many who feel strongly about the good they are doing, and have a desire to see the mission through. Conversely, there are countless examples of soldiers in the Revolution and the Civil War griping about their officers, the lack of proper equipment and, most notably, that people on the homefront are tired of the war and seem to have forgotten them. Even during World War II. One soldier wrote to his wife in May 1944, a full year before the war was won: 'By the way, if you want to do some real good back home, every time you hear somebody say that the war will be over soon, look them straight in the eye and tell them that a lot of people are still dying over here.'

"Other patterns emerge as well," Carroll continued. "There are two themes running through wartime correspondences that are absolute opposites. One is the soldiers' attempt, and I think it's quite poignant, to comfort those at home and downplay the danger they are in, perhaps even making light of it. 'This isn't half as scary as driving with Dad in his new car,' one jokes. 'Don't worry. Everything's fine.' The writers can't bear to imagine those back home fretting, pacing the floor.

"There is another impulse, however, and that is to tell everything that is going on, no matter how troubling it might be. Letter-writing can be cathartic, and it's not that the soldiers want their families to worry, but that their emotions get so bottled up they simply have to let them out. Compared to any other type of letter, war letters are the most intense. They become not only a tangible connection to loved ones back home, but also a soldier's own, ongoing chronicle of what it's like to face death."

We will see some venting and much brave, kindhearted stoicism in the letters from Iraq. As Carroll said, it has ever been so. On February 3, 1776, Joseph Hodgkins, a Continental officer, wrote to his wife, Sarah, in Ipswich, Mass.:

"My Dear I take this oppertunity to inform you that I am will att Presant . . . [W]e Live in our tent yet only when we are smoked out and then we git shealter some whare Else we live Pretty well and our Duty is not hard."

In fact, the Continental Army was constantly under duress during the war, and it is highly likely that Hodgkins's duty was very hard indeed. It should be said, the difficult effort to maintain a cheerful front was always mutual; this is from Sarah, writing to Joseph, 17 days later: "My Dear I take this oppertunity to write aline or two to inform you that we are all in a Comfortable State of Health through the goodness of God & I hope these lines will find you posest of the Same Blessing."

U.S. Army Lieutenant Robert Mitchell's letter to Winifred Bostwick in October 1918 was

Oct 6, 1918

A war letter written on April 16, 1944, by a very famous soldier, General Dwight D. Eisenhower, to his wife, Mamie, well illustrates that those at war are deeply concerned for those on the home-front—at all moments.

"[I]t is a terribly sad business to total up the casualties each day," Eisenhower wrote. "A man must develop a veneer of callousness that lets him consider such things dispassionately; but he can never escape a recognition of the fact that back home the news brings anguish and suffering to families all over the country. Mothers, fathers, brothers, sisters, wives and friends must have a difficult time preserving any comforting philosophy and retaining any belief in the eternal rightness of things. War demands real toughness of fiber—not only in the soldiers that must endure, but in the homes that must sacrifice their best."

The homes visited in this book, and in the HBO/*New York Times* documentary of the same name that will premiere on Veterans Day, November 11, 2004, are just such homes. Some are homes where the military tradition runs deep. Others are homes where the sacrifice is, to the survivors, new and unfathomable. They are homes where the horrible message has been delivered: that a son, daughter, parent or spouse is dead—and where letters already received, and some few still to come, take on an entirely new weight.

For there is one kind of war letter that has a greater potency than any other, and that is the last letter home. The reader approaches it with the knowledge that life has been lost, that a relationship between the son, daughter or spouse, and the parent, wife or husband has been most painfully rent. Private Elijah Beeman of the Union Army wrote to his sister, Ann, on April 26, 1862, "Truly we know not the horrors of war till peace has fled." He was killed five months later. The reader is hesitant to conjure but must do so: What horrors did Beeman experience before he wrote, what horrors in the interim and, finally, what horror claimed him?

It is hoped and intended that this is neither a pro- nor antiwar book. But it is inescapable that this is a sometimes difficult and painful book. What makes these letters so powerful, and to some people unapproachable, is the nature of war. It is not enough to say that war is a noble enterprise or a nasty business. War puts our brothers and sisters, sons and daughters, in places where those of us who have never experienced war cannot ever go. And from these other places, they write to us, and tell us what it is like. If they are taken from us, the letter stands as their final testament.

Consider how buoyant Lieutenant Robert F. Mitchell was on October 6, 1918, when he wrote to Winifred Bostwick.

"Sitting on head of cot, map case on knee and head ducked beneath canvas leanto against side of company officer's wagon. The war news continues to be the best ever. We're licking the tar out of the Germans and I'm a live part of it. The spirit of the boys is great and they are brimming over with confidence. These are stirring times and regardless of my personal outcome I'm glad to be a part of it." Lieutenant Mitchell was killed nine days later.

"I like to sit up these warm bright nights and watch the white clouds and dark shadows move," Lieutenant Jack Emery wrote to his fiancée, Audrey Taylor, on July 6, 1944. "That's when I miss you the most darling. On the nights that I sit up alone I can feel you very close to me. Sometimes we sit and talk and sometimes I pretend we are just sitting there with our arms about each other. Best I don't dwell on the subject just now cause I miss you so much right now it seems as though my heart is going to burst." Lieutenant Emery was killed when shot down over Burma three days later.

"Well Mother I am in a fox hole writing this letter," wrote Private William Geary from the Pusan Perimeter in Korea on September 6,

cheerful bordering on joyous. He said he was glad to be part of the fight, come what may.

1950—the day of his 22nd birthday. "I am still hear on the front line. I praye ever night. How is the family getting along fine I hope so. Well I will sent my birthday on the front line. It look like it. I am on a machine gun. I haven't no sleep for 6 days. Well Mother will close hoping to hear from you. Your loving son Bill." Private Geary was killed nine days after writing.

"Please disregard any small note of flippancy that might reveal itself in this letter," wrote Lance Corporal Thomas P. Noonan Jr. from Vietnam on October 17, 1968, to his sister and brother-in-law. "I try to avoid it, but when one is having such a good time it is hard not to be cheerful. I've thrown off the shackles of silly society. I've cast out my razor, divorced my soap, buried my manners, signed my socks to a two-year contract, and proved that you don't have to come in out of the rain. I scale the mountains, swim the rivers, soar through the skies in magic carpet helicopters. My advent is attended by Death and I've got chewing gum stuck in my mustache. I beat the draft." Noonan was killed within four months, and was posthumously awarded the Congressional Medal of Honor.

In that same war, on July 25, 1967, Airman Third Class Robert Zwerlein, who was at the time John McCain's plane captain, wrote to a friend in Port Washington, N.Y.: "Hi, Sue, This letter comes to you LIVE from Yankee Station, Gulf of Tonkin. Today we finally started flying missions against North Viet Nam and in about an hour we'll stop flying for 12 hours. So far we've lost no aircraft or even had one damaged. But, this is just the first day. Two pilots from my squadron were the first to drop bombs on N.V.N. from this carrier and they blew up a bridge. Beginners luck I guess! . . .

"Ya know Sue, the night before we pulled out of the Philippines to leave for Yankee Station some guys and I went to the club for a couple (80 or 90) drinks. Well, as you probably know there are guys from all over the USA and as it always happens the band would play DIXIE and all the guys from the south would start singing and yelling and cursing the Yankees from the north and the same thing would happen when the band would play Yankee Doodle only we got up. But as soon as that band started to play God Bless America, everyone, no matter where they were from, just stood up and started to sing. It was really great. It made me feel real good. I wish the people back home could have seen it.

"I imagine a lot of them would just say it was a bunch of drunken sailors that didn't even know what they were singing. But it wasn't that at all. It was a bunch of guys that are proud of their country and will fight and die if necessary for it. That's a lot more than I can say for some people in our country. Now, it may seem like I copied this out of books or something but I didn't and its just as it really happened and that's how I feel."

Four days after writing, Airman Zwerlein was engulfed in flames after an electrical charge accidentally launched a missile from a fighter jet on the deck of the USS *Forrestal*. The missile hit the fuel tank of a nearby airplane and exploded, setting off a chain reaction. (The plane's 31-year-old pilot, McCain, miraculously survived.) Zwerlein, with burns over 80 percent of his body, died on Aug. 1, 1967—one of 134 who were killed in the *Forrestal* fire.

The letters immediately preceding, written by soldiers soon to perish, were selected by Andrew Carroll for his book *War Letters,*

and he said of them, "What makes last letters so heartbreaking is not just 'hearing' the voices of the individuals who wrote them and knowing that they have been silenced forever, but realizing the pain of the intended recipients, the loved ones who originally read these letters when they arrived in the mail. In one of the most terrible ironies of war, these messages—so full of life and assurances that all is well—often come after the families have been notified that their soldier or Marine or airman or sailor is already dead."

Such was the case for Theodore Roosevelt, whose youngest son, Quentin, died in aerial combat on July 14, 1918. The Roosevelts received a flood of condolence, and the former President responded in handwritten script to a Mrs. Harvey L. Freeland:

"It is hard to open the letters coming from those you love who are dead; but Quentin's last letters, written during his three weeks at the front, when of his squadron on an average a man was killed every day, are written with real joy in the 'great adventure.' He was engaged to a very beautiful girl, of very fine and high character; it is heartbreaking for her, as well as for his mother; but they both said that they would rather have him never come back than never have gone. He had his crowded hour, he died at the crest of life, in the glory of the dawn. My other three boys are just as daring; and if the war lasts they will all be killed unless they are so crippled as to be sent home." The three remaining Roosevelt sons survived World War I, and they all served again in World War II—although only Archie would return alive this time.

Teddy Roosevelt knew the pain of receiving the news, then receiving the letter. Many of the families who now bravely present themselves to you know that same pain. Some of them share Roosevelt's conviction that it was better for their loved one to have fought, and some do not. Some of them are angry; all of them are proud. And, of course, all of them grieve. Their thoughts and emotions may be implicit, but are not the subject of this book.

Explicit are the voices of those who served their country honorably and died for what most of them felt was a just cause. What follows is what they said, in their last letters home.

The unchanging ritual: A solitary serviceman finds a quiet moment in the cacophony of war to share his thoughts and feelings. Bottom, in the Korean War; top left, in Vietnam; top right, during the first Gulf War in 1990.

The Troops

Pfc. Rachel Bosveld, Army
November 7, 1983 – October 26, 2003

Capt. Joshua Byers, Army
April 15, 1974 – July 23, 2003

Sgt. Frank Carvill, Army
December 11, 1952 – June 4, 2004

L. Cpl. Marcus Cherry, Marines
December 1, 1985 – April 6, 2004

2d Lt. Leonard Cowherd, Army
August 6, 1981 – May 16, 2004

Pvt. Robert Frantz, Army
December 8, 1983 – June 17, 2003

Pfc. Jesse Givens, Army
March 11, 1969 – May 1, 2003

S. Sgt. Stephen Hattamer, Army
January 19, 1960 – December 25, 2003

Pfc. Raheen Heighter, Army
December 8, 1980 – July 24, 2003

Pfc. Francisco Martinez-Flores, Marines
January 5, 1982 – March 25, 2003

Spc. Holly McGeogh, Army
August 29, 1984 – January 31, 2004

Capt. Pierre Piché, Army
September 10, 1974 – November 15, 2003

Spc. Robert Wise, Army
August 6, 1982 – November 12, 2003

Spc. Michelle Witmer, Army
February 13, 1984 – April 9, 2004

Pfc. Rachel Bosveld, Army

To her family she was "Sweetpea," and to her father she was "a chosen child," an unexpected blessing in their lives.

In the 1980s Marvin and Mary Bosveld of Waupun, Wis., serving as foster parents, took in Rachel as a neglected baby. They already had a son of their own, Craig, and now their family seemed complete. Life, of course, takes turns, and the Bosvelds separated. Rachel, who would remain devoted to both of her parents and would grow to idolize Craig, went to live with her mom in nearby Oshkosh.

She was a playful and talented child with an artistic bent. She loved to draw, particularly scenes of life outdoors. She was athletic, popular and single-minded. After her sophomore year at Oshkosh West High School, she moved back to Waupun to live with her father in his modest white house and to attend Waupun High. She made new friends instantly. She joined the drama club. She played Frieda in *You're a Good Man, Charlie Brown*. Her aspiration was to become a graphic artist. But first, there was something she had to do.

Upon graduating from high school in June 2002, Rachel made clear her determination to follow her father and brother into military service. Her dad had served in the Army in Italy in the 1960s and, years later, Craig had been posted in Alaska. Rachel's mother was desperate to dissuade her, but Rachel was resolute: "I know, Mom, but I have to do this . . . I want to keep up the family tradition. Except, Mom, I'm going to be the first girl in our entire family."

She graduated from boot camp in October 2002; Marvin rode his Harley from Wisconsin to Fort Leonard Wood in Missouri to watch the ceremony.

Rachel's assignment was with the Military Police in Germany, and that took her to Iraq in early 2003. Shortly after she arrived, she let her father know that she was prepared to "kick butt." But as time wore on, her ferocity eroded. Private Bosveld's eight-month tour of duty was harrowing even before its tragic conclusion: On September 12, the humvee in which she was riding was hit by a grenade. Trying to escape a fire inside the vehicle, Bosveld suffered a dislocated shoulder and strained neck—but did get the door open, only to find herself and others in her unit under small arms fire. She and her comrades survived the incident. Bosveld was awarded a Purple Heart, which no doubt made her proud, but after eight months in the desert she confided to her father, "More and more people want us to go home. Believe me, we want to go home."

She tried to downplay her brush with death in letters to her mother, but in a longer account to her brother, Craig, she graphically expressed the riot of emotions she felt during the attack. After recovering from her injuries, she returned to work, though she requested a switch to day duty from night—for safety's sake. Her principal assignment was to help guard a police station adjacent to the now notorious prison in Abu Ghraib, outside Baghdad.

Bosveld wrote regularly to her mother, father and brother right up to October 26, 2003, the day she was fatally injured during a mortar attack in Abu Ghraib. Her mother, in fact, would receive three of Rachel's letters two days after her daughter was killed. One said, "Mom, don't worry so much about me."

The letters that follow reveal more of what Rachel Bosveld wanted her loved ones to know.

Opposite: Mary Bosveld in Tucson, where she has relocated, and where a portrait of her daughter adorns a side table (above).

mom,   14OCTO

    Im doing fine mom. Yes I did get into
a sort of accident if thats what you want
to call it. We were hit by an IED OR RPG
which set our truck on fire because it
struck the battery and fuel line when
it exploded. I gave Craig as many details
as I could, if he wants to tell you more
he can. Im okay. My neck and shoulde
were pretty banged up for about two
weeks. My shoulder popped and
jammed my neck as well. I lost heari
in my left ear for a few weeks. My
hearing in general isnt great anymore
Ive been through and around my shou

Bosvelds,

This is a story I only want to write one time; so Craig, I'm sending it to you, in faith that you will share it with Mom and Dad and whomever else you wish.

A few days ago, the 12th of Sep around 0500, to be exact, myself and 5 others were patrolling the area of our old IP (Iraqi Police) station. It was a quiet evening, probably too quiet. My vehicle was the lead vehicle in our two vehicle convoy. We were hit by an armor-piercing RPG (rocket-propelled grenade). It must have struck our fuel line because almost instantly our entire vehicle was in flames. There was fire and smoke everywhere. At first we thought we were hit by an IED (improvised explosive device). It was loud, there was shouting, my team-leader's seat was on fire. I found my seatbelt but it was stuck. Damn it, I knew I shouldn't have worn it. I told myself several times that it would be the death of me. Not panicking, I continued to work at getting it loose.

The fire grew, my team-leader's beside me now yelling something. He couldn't get his door, pleading for me to hurry. Where's my gunner? Pulling, pushing, yes finally. Okay, the door . . . Just my luck, a 400-lb door is stuck. First the seat belt now this. More shouting. Seems so far away, like a voice at the end of a tunnel. Got to get the door open or we're going to die. Where's my gunner? I close my eyes and throw myself into the door. Still doesn't budge. This is it. This is how I am going to die. No! I open my eyes and throw myself once more. Oh Thank God, it opened. I'm stuck. My seatbelt's all wrapped up in my LBV (load-bearing vest). Hurry, I gotta hurry. Once we're out, we stop to see if we're all okay. Everything's a blur. Now what?, what was that? Someone's shooting at us. Go, go, go. No rifle, it's in the truck. Go, go. Back at the station we get another unit to escort us to a military medical facility. No one got shot but the gunner's bleeding. Gotta hurry. I'm okay, right.

I didn't really plan to write it that way. You should see the remain of our truck. Bagby, my gunner, had two shrapnel wounds, my team-leader has one, I have none. Though I did pop my shoulder trying to get the door open. It's badly bruised and my neck's pretty stiff. I have had a constant headache since then. I throw up everything that I eat. The doctor said I popped my shoulder and that muscles are spasming. I'll be sore, stiff, and bruised for a while. I lost all hearing in my left ear. Should come back in about 7 days. Didn't pop my eardrums or anything. They put me on some meds that relax my muscles so I sleep about 16 hours of the 24-hour day. I'm okay though. I want you all to know that I'm okay . . .[the letter continues on the following page]

Fortunately, two days prior to the attack we got our M1114 . . . back. Had we been in our old soft-shell we'd be dead. Miracles do happen. That truck has a total of two weeks and two days of this war, but it saved our lives. Whoever did it was there and saw us walk away from it. They won't win. After it happened an informer went into the IP station and said there had been a planned attack because of Sep 11th. He directed them to 3 other IEDs on the same road. We'd have been hit no matter what that night.

I was able to get pictures of our truck. Everything was melted or destroyed. When they lifted it to put it on a flat bed to bring it back for inventory and investigation, you could see a perfectly shaped rectangle where the frame melted to the road. They found some melted remains of my M-4 barrel, nods (night observation devices), and something really strange. I had a personal bag with a notebook in it. Everything in the truck was ruined except for my notebook with a letter to Dad, one for Mom, and one to Craig and Family. Strange huh? Unfortunately when they found the notebook they threw it away, but it was still strange. Everything in the vehicle was melted or charred. Maybe it's a sign, telling me how many great things I have.

Well, that's all for now. Oh, so that you aren't worrying (Mom), the Commander is giving us his vehicle to use whenever we go out on missions. I've been issued another M-4 and will soon be getting issued everything else I lost. Oh, and Mom, your package had great timing, my cd player and cds were burned. Thank you all for your love and support.

Rachel

* * * * *

Mom,

Hey mom how are you? I'm doing great this week. Sure, I've dodged lots of bullets and such, gotten little to no sleep, and eaten nasty food, but I'm doing great.

I got to drive a tank! . . . Learned how to operate everything, load everything, and I got to DRIVE IT!

I'm getting a Purple Heart for the accident. Someone is always getting injured here. There have been no fatalities so far in my company, though, just lots of injuries . . . Eighteen days till my birthday! I can't wait! . . . Just wanted to let you know I'm O.K., and I miss you.

I love you,
Rachel

Opposite: Her mother's walls. Above: Rachel's father carries the folded flag that honors a veteran.

Private Bosveld's second Purple Heart was awarded posthumously to her family. She was buried in Berlin, Wis., on November 7, 2003—a day that would have been her 20th birthday.

Capt. Joshua Byers, Army

Josh often cited this passage from the Bible in his

correspondence: "I can do all things through Christ which strengtheneth me." The quotation was from Paul's letter to the Philippians. It sustained the deeply devout Joshua Byers in times of trouble.

He was the oldest of three boys born to Lloyd and Mary Byers, Southern Baptist missionaries who handed down their faith. (His brothers, Milam and Jared, are members of the popular Christian rock band, Bleach, whose most recent disc, *Astronomy,* is inspired in part by Josh's life and death.) Lloyd and Mary, seeking to start a new church, moved the family from Anderson, S.C. to Sparks, Nev., just east of Reno, in 1989. Josh was in his freshman year of high school. Such a move would be difficult for any teenager, and it was tough for him. But he was determined not to let the disruption get him down. He set his sights on several goals, one short-term, the others long-term. First, he wanted to become the student body president at Reed High School. Then, he wanted to attend one of the country's top military academies and serve in whatever capacity that entailed, enter the U.S. Senate and, finally, become President of the United States. Those who knew him thought everything was possible.

The race for student body president at Reed was not simply a popularity contest. In the predominantly Mormon city of Sparks, whoever was elected to lead the student body was automatically awarded a full scholarship to Brigham Young University. Josh—a relative newcomer, a Southern Baptist, the son of a minister—looked like an exotic, vying for such a prize. Yet in 1991 he became the first non-Mormon to win the presidency in the school's 17-year history. Battalion Commander of Reed's JROTC as well, Josh had outstanding grades—no surprise—and was accepted at all three major military academies. His guidance counselor at Reed, Bob White, told a reporter from the *Reno Gazette-Journal* that Josh chose West Point and the Army because he thought "their honor code is better."

Josh (top, left) with his brothers, and in Iraq with his mail. Opposite: Milam, Mary, Jared and Lloyd in Guam, where the parents are on their latest mission.

Do not misinterpret here: Josh was not just about drive, ambition and dutiful Christianity—although those aspects were certainly parts of his character. A cut-up, he loved to joke around with friends, often using a hand-held video camera to do riffs on *Saturday Night Live* skits, or to lip-synch favorite songs.

At West Point, Josh was elected Executive Officer of the Cadet Honor Committee, a distinction that he took very seriously. David Roberts, a cadet who graduated two years behind Byers in 1998, respected him "for choosing to uphold standards instead of garner favor. The impression he left on me was one of being strict and yet fair."

After West Point, Josh's course was a rising arc of success. He was assigned to Kuwait for six months in 1998. In December of that year, he married Kim Redfearn, also the child of a Baptist minister, whom he had met while visiting friends in Hartselle, Ala. He also completed his Officer Advanced Course, earning a Master's degree in engineering. In 2001, he was assigned to the General's Staff at Fort Carson, Colo., and he and Kim settled in nearby Fountain.

Josh was deployed to Iraq in April 2003 with the Second Squadron, Third Armored Cavalry Regiment. By every account, he was brave and dedicated in the field of war. Once, spotting an Iraqi child who had wandered into a minefield in search of firewood, Josh calmly wove his way through the live mines and brought the child out. On the Fourth of July, to provide some diversion for his unit, he bought live chickens and he and his men dressed them up and raced them.

He was, on July 23, 2003, the 29-year-old commander of Fox Troop, a unit of 100 soldiers riding Bradley Fighting Vehicles and other tanks. On that day, which was only 40 days after Byers's dream of commanding a troop came true, he and his unit were attacked while traveling not far from Baghdad in a convoy of about 50 vehicles. Two men detonated an explosive device right next to Byers's humvee, killing him instantly.

While completely committed to his mission, Josh Byers was also aware of the challenges and dangers that his posting presented. He expressed these thoughts plainly in letters to his parents.

Dear Mom & Dad,

21 JUL 03
AR Ramadi,
IRAQ

Hey! I'm doing well - healthy & safe so far in Iraq after about 4 months. I received another package from you yesterday along with a letter from Dad. You go above & beyond for me, your support is amazing - I am so thankful for you. You don't need to send so much - but everything you send gets used by me or a soldier that needs it more than me. ☺

Dad's letter was so great to read - it was typed, so it looks like you're getting used to the computer, Dad! Both of your letters are so comforting - it feels so great to come in dirty & sweaty from a mission to a letter, or letters sometimes, laying on my cot. I hope Kim & I can one day be half the parents you are.

It sounds like Guam is awesome from your letters. Sounds like the need there is so great too, that you are fulfilling a great need there for the missionaries, pastors & lay-people on the islands. I loved reading what you wrote about the young Chinese girls who work in the sweat shops and their love for Christ. I can't wait to come & see you in Guam and meet as many of these people as possible!

We conducted a huge operation in the desert about a week ago. We had intel that suggested that the bad guys were hiding weapons & ammo out in the desert & bringing it into the city to attack us. We swept all of the desert north of Al Ramadi & found lots of weapons/ammo. Very successful! Just yesterday (2 days after coming in from the desert), we conducted a raid on a some leaders/members of a group called the Noor Mohammed Group. Bad dudes - smuggling arms from Syria & conducting attacks on U.S. Troops. We captured all of the targets we were after & lots of weapons. 2 of the targets that we captured (Fox Troop) turned out to be 1st cousins of Saddam Hussein. We found all kinds of Saddam stuff in their house. We have good intel that Saddam has hidden in this house over the past 2 months... Wouldn't it be great if we caught the big fish! Wow! Ha! It's possible! I think I'd probably get my chance to be on Jay Leno if that happened! Ya think?! Ha!

I haven't heard from Milan or Javelin in a little while but understand they've finished recording their new album - I can't wait to hear it! I miss them very much. I can't wait until the next time the whole family is together!

I love you both with all of my heart! I'm working very hard here - adding honor to our country and to our family name! As they say in Georgia, "I ain't skeered." We're fighting our way home! I love you both! I miss you!

Love

Hey Mom and Dad,

Things are going OK, relatively speaking here. Still plenty of danger, unfortunately, but rest assured we are taking all precautions possible and "givin' 'em hell!!"
I see more courage in a day than I could ever have imagined before this. You inspire
me to keep on going out here. You've made it so much easier for me to see the big
picture as I go through life: That service to God and others is what matters.

Speaking of service, my next big opportunity of service is finally here. A couple
of days ago . . . my Squadron Commander told me that I would be taking command of Fox
Troop in June . . . I left my conversation with him walking on air!

Not only will I soon be a Cavalry Troop Commander . . . but I will have the opportunity and the incredible responsibility of commanding in combat. I have to admit
that I am really nervous and just pray that I am up to the task out here to lead 120
men in combat operations. I will give them everything I have to give. I love them
already, just because they're mine. I pray, with all my heart, that I will be able
to take every single one of them home safe when we finish our mission here.

Love,
JT

* * * * *

Dear Mom + Dad,

I received a care package from you a couple of days ago! It was huge! Plenty of
baby wipes, razors, a snowboard game for the gameboy, PECANS, gatorade, <u>everything</u>
I could possibly need.

Thank you so much. Thank you, thank you, thank you. I can't tell how much it means
to me that you would continually go to such effort to support me here. I have heard
that the two greatest things in life are to love and to be loved. I know both because
of you.

Love,
JT

Dear Mom + Dad,

It's another hot (115°, I think.), dust-filled gut-check of a day . . . In the past two nights we've been attacked by RPGs [rocket-propelled grenades] each night while on patrol. No casualties for us, but last night we got the group who shot at us!

We are accomplishing our mission here + I think I'll take a lot of pride in that for the rest of my life. Although the sacrifice is great, the rewards of service are so much greater. God has shown me things I could never have seen if I weren't in this position, in this time.

Love,
JT

* * * * *

Dear Mom + Dad,

Life here continues to be challenging, but we're all hanging in there. We got a blow to our morale a few days ago when the Corps Commander visited us . . . He said there was no way we were going home in less than 9-12 months . . . We're working on month #4 right now and it already seems like we've been here forever + a day.

We're supposed to start transitioning to "engagement with the local populous" or "winning hearts + minds" work. So far, they've only seen the tough, aggressive side of us. Now, we're supposed to go out + give them school supplies, clothes, sports equipment, help restore electricity, purify water, etc. I'll be going out this morning with a bunch of soccer balls to give to kids.

We conducted a raid on an Islamic extremist's house . . . a few days ago . . . I was wrapped up in the situation . . . I looked across the lawn and saw one of my soldiers calming down a little girl (probably 2 or 3 years old)—cute as a button + crying her head off—as you can imagine. We get one candy bar a week (on average) . . . and he was giving her his candy bar, feeding it to her a piece at a time until she stopped crying. He did that just moments after being shot at and shooting men in this girl's house, probably her Dad and brothers/cousins. It really touched me.

Love,
JT

The date of his death—July 23—was his mother's birthday. She was flying with her husband from Guam, where they were working as missionaries, to Atlanta, for what they thought would be a family visit. Milam and Jared were waiting for them at the airport with the devastating news.

Joshua Byers was posthumously awarded the Bronze Star and a Purple Heart. On August 2, 2003 he was interred in Mountville, S.C.

Josh's widow, Kim, accepts the flag during a memorial service. His parents sit beside her.

Sgt. Frank Carvill, Army

His family had worried before.

On September 11, 2001, Frank Carvill's brother, sister and mother sat tensely in the family home in Carlstadt, N.J., desperately hoping to hear from Frank, a paralegal working for the Port Authority of New York and New Jersey in the North Tower of the World Trade Center. His siblings could see the billowing plumes of smoke 12 miles east across the Hudson River as they fretted. Frank did call; he had been on the street when he saw the first plane hit. He came home on that day and also the day of the 1993 terrorist attack on the Twin Towers—a morning when he helped carry a disabled co-worker down 54 flights of stairs. But he would not return from Iraq.

Frank T. Carvill was born on December 11, 1952, the first of four children to Irish immigrants Dan and Mary. Dan had worked as a mason, and he built the house in Carlstadt himself. Frank fulfilled his part of the American Dream equation by graduating from Rutgers University. His major was political science, and it was politics, as well as his Irish American heritage, that informed him. He was a founding member of the Irish Immigration Reform Movement in the 1980s, active in his local Ancient Order of Hibernians, and also served as treasurer of the Emerald Isle Immigration Center. It is fair to say that, at the time of his death, he was one of the best-known movers and shakers in New York City's energetic Irish American community.

At Rutgers, his status as a student had allowed him to avoid the military draft, but he did want to serve his country and so, in 1984, he enlisted in the Army National Guard and stayed in for two decades. Carvill found himself, in 2003, on the verge of decisions, as events had caused shifts in his life. His father died in 1996, and he moved from the city back home to help his brother Daniel take care of his mother, who is legally blind. Then his other brother Mike died in 2003 of cancer, which, of course, caused everyone in the family not only to grieve but also to reconsider the immediate future. And finally, Frank's long relationship with Monalisa Forde of Jersey City seemed headed for the altar. Frank told friends that he was thinking of retiring from the Guard after 20 years. But then, in March of 2003, his unit was activated. Carvill, as his mother's main support, could have opted out of Iraq. But he didn't. How could he not go, he told his buddies, when married men and women were fighting and dying over there?

Frank's unit, Third Battalion, 112th Field Artillery, shipped out from Fort Dix, N.J. to Iraq in February, 2004. His two principal assignments in Baghdad were as a driver or gunner in a convoy of humvees that trucked supplies around the city. In dozens of letters and e-mails to friends and relatives—longtime pals Rick Rancitelli and Steve Zurier, sister Peggy Liguori, young nephews Danny and Drew, friend and colleague Kathy Collins and others—he calmly painted pictures of what was clearly a difficult situation. On June 2 he told the kids how he wished he were visiting them just then, but had lost his scheduled leave. To the adults he talked candidly about the prison-abuse scandal at Abu Ghraib.

"All is well here, at least for now," he wrote to his sister-in-law Andrea Carvill. "However this is a very unpredictable and potentially dangerous place."

On June 4, 2004, the convoy in which Carvill was riding came under attack on Palestine Street in Baghdad near the Shiite district of Sadr City. Five U.S. soldiers were killed, five wounded. Back in New Jersey, Carvill's sister, Peggy, was preparing a meal for herself and her husband, Joe, when she heard the TV report. God, she thought, how terrible. Even then the doorbell rang, and when she saw that it was a colonel and a chaplain, she knew that Frank, who was 51, had died.

In one of his last letters home, Frank Carvill, a man with many friends, told Rancitelli he was looking forward to their long-planned trip to Civil War battlefields, to honor those dead. "Good men all," he wrote.

From top: Carvill in Iraq; Mary smiles at her boy; Danny and Drew during an outing with their uncle. Opposite: Carvill's sister Peggy, mother Mary and brother-in-law Joe, are a family that has suffered much in recent years.

Steve,

I am at a complete loss as to what happened with regard to the prisons. The guys I work with simply don't understand what caused this to occur.

We are a National Guard unit. Many of the guys are older, with families and simply want to do the tour and go home. No one in my unit would have anything to do with what those idiots did. We give candy to kids, purchase items in the local economy and return accurate and well-aimed fire upon legitimate targets when fired upon.

Meanwhile, the days plod on and summer rapidly approaches. Quite frankly, I think the worst position to be in is to be a parent of a young person who is deployed. Any normal person worries about their kids, even if they are simply in school. Can you imagine if [either of your sons], Ben or Sol, were in Baghdad or Mosul, with a forward element of the Army or Marines? Or, if my brother's kids, Danny or Drew, were similarly situated? (Do something with the boys this summer, before they realize you are not cool.) This experience has been good to teach the simple truth: "There is no place like home." Everybody wants to go home.

Frank

* * * * *

Dear Danny and Drew,

Thank you very much for your beautiful book and drawings. I enjoyed reading it very much. The drawings were very good also. Drew, you did a nice job in your drawing also. Dan, I enjoyed seeing the rabbit (is that Hoppy?) running around after the carrot. Drew, you did a very fine drawing of flowers and a tree. It was colorful and very well done.

I was going to visit you in June but at the last minute, we had news that one of my fellow soldiers had a death in his family. He had to go back to America right away so he took my seat on the airplane. However, as soon as I can get leave (that's what they call vacation in the military), then I will come visit you guys and your mom. When you are in the Army, Uncle Sam is the boss. "Uncle Sam" is the nickname for the United States (US).

I really miss you guys and can't wait to see you both. You are still my BEST Buddies and we will have fun when I come to Florida! . . . Be good, guys, and be careful. Watch out for cars when you are riding your bikes.

I love you guys very much. God Bless,

Frank

Rick,

Many thanks for your care package. All the contents will be put to good use.

It is not possible to be candid in the e-mails because of security checks and regs. Too many guys have sent detailed messages, which we think have been accessed by the bad guys. I have nothing on that order of magnitude, but it is easier to write even though you can barely read my writing.

The city of Baghdad is very interesting. Without this little war, it would be fun to cruise around town. Maybe I'm still a naive liberal, but I don't feel paranoid here, at least during the day. The city itself is busy and very oriented towards business. There are stores everywhere. Thousands of tiny shops selling everything.

The older sections of town are the most interesting. You can see tiny alleyways with shops, crowded apartment buildings, dogs, kids, women in traditional clothing, sheep butchers in the streets, sheep herders in the street, horse and donkey carts, disassembled appliances, cars, etc.

Most of the guys are scared of the older neighborhood because you're not able to move a Humvee as quickly through the crowded streets. Maybe they are right. There is great paranoia over IEDs (improvised explosive devices), which are out there. RPGs (rocket-propelled grenades) are around as well, but IEDs are the big worries. Our guys have been hit by both IEDs and RPGs, but no major injuries to date. The trucks have held up well, but the ordinance against them has been relatively small. If you run into a a anti-tank mine or an artillery shell, then you might have a problem.

I wish none of this were necessary. Most of the time we come and go without incident, but the risk is always here, so you can never relax. I can't wait to get out of here and get out of uniform.

All the paranoia in the Army is incredible. I am not supposed to talk about our operations. Get rid of this letter.

Looking forward to a cold beer at your new house.

Frank

Hello Kathy,

Thanks for your letter. Sorry it took so long to respond. We are living in a large fortified US Army base just southeast of Baghdad. It has the basic amenities but is still a big, dusty Army camp.

We have been busy here, with most of our time being spent with the Iraqi police, as we try and help them become a more professional force.

I know the prison abuse scandal has produced a political firestorm at home. Everybody I know is at a loss to explain what happened. We don't work with prisoners, except those in holding cells in the police stations. None of it makes any sense. We have people risking their lives on a regular basis who see this as a disaster and as some thing that defies explanation.

I cannot assess the overall situation here. The US cannot afford to "lose." Losing is defined as leaving without a stable government in place which can be described as non-hostile. In the interim, we have to continue to absorb the <u>huge</u> financial cost and the horrible numbers of dead and wounded.

Good luck with your practice and say hello to everyone.

All the best,
Frank Carvill

CARLSTADT N.J.
Community Calendar

BOROUGH OF CARLSTADT
EXTENDS IT'S
PATHY AND PRAYERS
O THE FAMILY OF
FRANK CARVILL
R FALLEN HERO

Funeral services for Sergeant Carvill were held at St. Joseph's Church in East Rutherford, N.J., on June 12, 2004. Hundreds gathered to say goodbye as bagpipes played. The "Celtic Song of Farewell" was sung. Carvill was buried at Brigadier General William C. Doyle Veterans Memorial Cemetery near Fort Dix.

L. Cpl. Marcus Cherry, Marines

"Dear Mrs. King," wrote Second Lieutenant V.S. Valdés from Kuwait to Marcus Cherry's mother in California on February 28, 2004, "I have the distinct pleasure and honor of being your son's platoon commander for Operation Iraqi Freedom II . . . This letter is a simple gesture on my part to show you just how much I appreciate the work you did in raising your son. The fact that Marcus is out here ready to go into Iraq speaks volumes of the values you instilled in him."

His mother was crucial in his life, and so was his stepfather, James Tyler. When Marcus graduated from Marine boot camp—no mean feat—he sent Mr. Tyler a picture of himself in full-dress uniform and a note: "Dear Dad, . . . I want to thank you for being there for me and participating in raising me to the best of your ability. I will do my best to make you proud and uphold the Corps values of Honor, Courage, and Commitment to Corps and Country. I'll see you later and take care."

The gesture and the sentiment expressed were typical. Marcus was a sweet, fun-loving person when he was growing up in Imperial, Calif., east of San Diego, a town where (and Marcus fully realized this) some kids turned out good and some went bad. Marcus, for his part, loved to change the color of his hair; when he was finally able to toy with a goatee or mustache, he did. But he was no rebel; he was playing around. He loved rapping—he was better than pretty good—and he carried the football for the Imperial High Tigers. He was handsome and popular, devoted to his family and friends. He fell in love with Shannon Severe, also of Imperial, and they dated for two and a half years. The couple became engaged.

When Marcus graduated from high school in 2003 he entered the military along with several classmates—Mike Sanders, Lee Paradise, Sam Selay. Marcus joined the Marines and told his mother that he wanted to prove something to himself. His older brother, Andre, was already a Marine and heading for Iraq, and Marcus would do the same. He was only 18 years old but a talented rifleman. "I am proud to have Marcus in First Platoon," wrote Lieutenant Valdés to Mrs. King.

Cherry's unit, the Second Battalion, Fourth Marines, arrived in Iraq in February of 2004. By spring, operating in the central part of the country, they were in the thick of the war. Marcus talked to Shannon on April 3 and confided that he wasn't getting a lot of sleep and that things seemed to be getting pretty scary with the insurgency. Still, he urged her to keep planning for their November wedding. One of the phrases he used was that death was not in his vocabulary.

But Cherry had been accurate in his assessment of the situation on the ground: In early April, coordinated uprisings and daily hostile fire were simply a way of life in Al Anbar province. And on April 6, Marcus Cherry, 18, was one of several Marines killed in combat in the city of Ramadi. "[His] squad went to rein-force a 4 man Scout Sniper team that was taking fire from a platoon sized enemy element," Valdés reported in a second letter to Mrs. King. "In the ensuing action, Marcus was killed by enemy gunfire. The ferocity and leadership that he displayed on this day and many others has proven to me that Lance Corporal Marcus Miguel Cherry is a hero." Valdés went on to call Cherry the "model Marine."

While in Iraq, Cherry wrote to his mother and to his half-siblings, Stephen and Monique Tyler. Among three quotes that he included at the end of an April 4 letter to Monique, a letter written within 48 hours of his death, is an especially plaintive, poignant and true phrase: "Only the dead have seen the end of war."

Marcus (above, left) is all smiles as he poses with his brother and fellow Marine, Andre. Opposite: He is survived by Andre, Stephen, Monique and his mother, Genevieve King.

Dear Mom,

I'm a Lance Corporal. I'm a Team Leader and about to be a Squad Leader. I'm pick-
ing up rather quick because of my capabilities to handle responsibilities. I know the
Marine Corps was the best decision for my life at the time I joined. It's a fast
way to grow up, but I was made for it. Statistically, the Infantry ages you 16 years
for every 4 years you stay in. I'll probably get out when I turn 21. Anyway,
mom, I'm doing good. What I want you to do is just be proud of your sons.

I love you,
Marcus

* * * * *

Dear Stephen,

Whats up bro? Sorry if I'm writing all slopy but all I have is a little flash
light and its pitch black out. I'm In a tower guarding our base. It realy late at
night . . . Thers a lot of kids here. When I see them I think of you. There always
asking for something. They say, "Mister Mister give me money" or "give me chocolate"
or "give me food" The kids here suffer a lot . . . I cant wait to get back home.
Pray for me that I'll be safe here okay. Be good Steve.

Love,
MARCUS

* * * * *

Dear Monique,

Whats up Miss Junior High? How have you been . . . Whats up with Stephen writing
to me and not you I know you like to write. You better not be writing to no boys at
school. Dont even try to lie either cuz I'll just look in your year book. I know
everyone writes everything in yearbooks. Dont worry, I was your age before. So how
are your grades . . . Do real good like me and you can . . . take college classes
like I did . . . You can worry about boys later . . . I love and miss you and Stephen.

Always,
Marcus

"BORN TO FIGHT, TRAINED TO KILL, READY TO DIE, NEVER WILL."
"No better friend no worse enemy"
"only the dead have seen the end of war"

At Camp Combat Outpost in Ramadi, Cherry's rifle and helmet commemorate him.

On Saturday, April 17, 2004, Lance Corporal Marcus Cherry's friends and family gathered at Christ Community Church in El Centro, Calif., to bid their loved one goodbye. "He brought life," said youth pastor James Whitehead during the services. "He brought charm." Shannon Severe read a poem for her late fiancé. Finally, at the burial at Evergreen Cemetery, there was a 21-gun salute. Doves were released, and they flew off into the California sky.

2d Lt. Leonard Cowherd, Army

Leonard's path was the right one.

In the Cowherd family there was no doubt about that. When Leonard graduated from the U.S. Military Academy at West Point in 2003, there was absolute pride for this, the latest son to extend a military tradition that dated back to colonial America.

Leonard M. Cowherd III—"Lenny"—was born on August 6, 1981, to Mary Ann and Leonard Cowherd of Culpeper, Va. His dad was a proud member of the Sons of the American Revolution, and the boy grew up well aware of duty to one's country. At Wakefield Country Day School in Rappahannock County, Lenny showed himself to be smart, intense and personable. He was West Point material.

He fell in love with a girl from back home, Sarah Cerri of Yorktown. She, Lenny and Lenny's identical twin brother, Charles, were three amigos, doing everything together. Sarah was also from a military family—her dad was ex-Army—and while Lenny was at the Academy she attended the Virginia Women's Institute for Leadership. She and Lenny married on June 28, 2003, a second happy ceremony in that season, hard on the heels of Lenny's graduation.

His extended assignment in Iraq, which began in January 2004, was as a platoon commander with Company C, First Battalion, 37th Armor Regiment, the First Armored Division—a tank corps. Cowherd was in charge of 16 men and four armored vehicles. Once he had settled into his mission, Cowherd was inspired to let the folks back home know of life on the battlefield—folks beyond his immediate family. "Hello, Culpeper!" he wrote in a column, one of three, that appeared in the *Culpeper Star-Exponent*. "This is Leonard Cowherd reporting from Northern Baghdad . . . Most of the members of my platoon have been here since late April or early May of last year. They have endured an incredible amount of hardships, in terms of living conditions, weather and difficult missions . . . My unit is currently living in what used to be a small amusement park known as Baghdad Island. Saddam Hussein diverted the Tigris River to create this small resort for him and his elite group of followers . . . Most Iraqis appear to live either in poverty or . . . how can I say it . . . even worse poverty. This is a situation we are trying to help. The roles that the American soldier must play are numerous: diplomat, traffic cop, judge, humanitarian assistant, and warfighter."

In a March 20 column, he focused again on the Iraqi citizenry, for which he had clear sympathy. "Despite their poverty, however, generosity and hospitality are strong characteristics of the Iraqi people. During a recent mission, a farmer brought out a pot of tea for myself and the soldiers in my vehicle, complete with saucers, tea cups, teaspoons and sugar."

At one point, he wrote of a chaotic village scene, "I make my way through the crowd toward the village leader with my hand resting on my holstered pistol. Another man comes right to me, puts his hand gently on my arm and says, 'There is no need for that. We are all friends here.'"

Of course there is always a need to be wary in a war zone, where it is never true that everyone's a friend. On the afternoon of Sunday, May 16, 2004, Cowherd was part of an operation attempting to secure a building near the Mukhayam Mosque in Karbala, 70 miles southwest of Baghdad, when he was hit in the chest by a sniper's bullet and killed. He was 22.

Second Lieutenant Cowherd left behind several different impressions of the war in Iraq—those he had shared with the readers of the *Star-Exponent,* and the following even more personal reflections that he sent to his family.

In an earlier uniform . . .

. . . with his twin, Charles . . .

. . . and on his wedding day. Opposite: The Cowherd family at home in Culpeper—Leonard's mother, Mary Ann, his brothers Charles and Colby, his father, Len, and his sister Laura.

Charles,

First thanks so much for orchestrating the movement of such a voluminous amount of mail in this direction. It has been incredible, although somewhat embarassing. I am going to save all of it, of course. I got a leter from Lizzie Williams + Maya W. I will have to let you read them when I get home—absolutely hilarious on the unintentional comedy scale, but also very thoughtful and heartfelt.

I've been going to church services whenever I can. There is a "contemporary service" at 8am and "traditional service" at 8pm on Sundays. I go to the latter—our Chaplain is of the Church of Nazarene—Dad would probably cringe every time he says "just" during his prayers. First, I would like for it to be completely taken off the record—any of my previous misgivings about you returning to St. G's for another year. I'm really jealous and dissapointed that I probably won't be able to visit. Attending services here are really valuable to my piece of mind. It's such a powerful experience, and so similar to St. George's—a small number of people from all over the world who don't know one another, dirty, tired, armed to the teeth, shuffle into a small tent with cement floors and poor lighting, worshipping with old beat-up bibles and a sheet of printed-out prayers. A small 20 ft by 20 ft square of the Body of Christ amidst a Muslim Nation. Last service, the chaplain brought a small book of songs and asked if we wanted to pick any—I chose "Be Glorified," which was great to hear although our rendition did not include my favorite part—when you stretch the title into five syllables.

Otherwise, the job is going well. The overwhelming focus at this point in time is to get eveyone home safe and sound. I wish that I knew more about my job—I am overwhelmed at times by its complexities and my utter lack of experience. It is always difficult being the new guy—and I suppose that it would have been more difficult had I "taken over" after our return to Germany.

Best wishes to eveyone, good luck in school and basketball.

Love,
Leonard

Sarah,

Today we got the word that a member of our comp[any]
[d]ied of wounds received from yesterday's fightin[g]
[it']s pretty much the universal reaction. I am asha[med]
[h]e wasn't a member of my platoon. We had a meet[ing]
[to] go where our batallion and company commander bri[efed]
[us]. As we walked in, I saw their platoon leader, D[o]
[n]y, a great role model, crying his eyes out. As we
[w]ent up to him with the impossible purpose of conso[ling]
[h]im that the one thing that he didn't want to happe[n]
[the thing] that I pray for every night - he lost one of [his men]
[h]ad absolutely the most helpless look on his face.
[Her]e Sarah - they are just kids. I'm not an old codger mysel[f]
~~but these guys~~ are going through the experiences that these [guys are at the]
[the] age of 18, 19, 20. My driver and my loader - they have [at]
[the] same time seen so much. If you saw them walki[ng]
[you wou]ld think that they belong in the arcade or a movie the[ater with]
[the]ir friends, getting in trouble doing stuff kids do

Sarah,

I truly have reached an impasse in my life, a great transition into something vastly different. I'm anxious, very happy, a little scared. A little wistful. Since the day I entered West Point . . . I have been waiting for this day, the day I would join a unit that had a specific job as part of an overall mission, where everyone helped each other achieve common goals—a basic change from me helping me, to me helping other people.

I love you, Baby,
Leonard

* * * * *

Sarah,

I barely knew the guy—maybe had seen him once or twice walking around. In the middle of the round stage, there was a pair of desert boots, an inverted M-16, a pair of dog tags hanging off his rifle. Two posthumous awards, Bronze Star and Purple Heart. . . Every person who talked about him mentioned the fact that he was always in the gym, always trying to get stronger. One of his friends said he once told him that he wanted to get bigger so that he could wrap his fiancé up in his arms and protect her from all the dangers in the world.

The service continued with a Roll Call. The deceased's name is called three times, echoing the fact that he is no longer with us . . . But the beauty and power of the ceremony perhaps disguised to a certain extent the underlying cause of his death—questions about why we are here, and on, and on. These questions should still be asked, but not at this time. I only hope that I will never have to attend one of these services again.

Love,
Leonard

* * * * *

Sarah,

Some of these guys out here, Sarah—they are just kids . . . If you saw them walking down the street, you would think they belong in the arcade or a movie theater, hanging out with their friends, getting in trouble, doing stuff kids do—not putting their lives on the line, every second of every day . . . [This last letter was unfinished at the time of Cowherd's death.]

Back in the United States, the news that the Army had lost a young man of great leadership potential was spread. Sarah was told at her parents' home in Yorktown, where she had been staying since Lenny's deployment. Up in Culpeper, 50 flags bloomed on Main Street. Further north, at the famous campus looming above the Hudson River, an announcement was made over breakfast to 4,000 assembled cadets, many of whom remembered Lenny. Cowherd was the 11th West Point graduate to be killed in Operation Iraqi Freedom.

On May 26, 2004, the Old Guard presided as the wooden casket bearing Second Lieutenant Cowherd was buried at Arlington National Cemetery outside Washington, D.C. A piper played "Amazing Grace," the family minister said prayers and 21 guns saluted the fallen officer. Finally, "Taps," and the flag was folded and presented to Sarah—the latest military honor in a family line that is as old as the country itself.

In the family home, a corner assemblage remembers Lenny. The folded flag is on the table. In the photograph on the wall, a soldier in Iraq salutes Cowherd and the two others who died.

Pvt. Robert Frantz, Army

Shannon changed everything. Robby Frantz was

leading one life, then he had a daughter, then he was leading another life.

The seeds for the epiphany that would come with parenthood were, perhaps, sown long ago. Robert L. Frantz, born in Alma, Mich. to Kim and Randy Joe in 1983, lost his own father to a car accident. He was only four years old. When his mother married Vincent Smith, a Lackland Air Force Base firefighter, Robby and his older sister, Heather, got a loving stepfather, but still Robby wondered if he might have turned out different with guidance from his late father who, as it happened, was an Army man.

It's not that Robby was a bad kid. It is, rather, that he was something of a perpetual kid—a kid's kid, a guy's guy. His life revolved around his buddies, which meant there was a near-constant search for fun and thrills. He was a footloose teen with an ear-to-ear smile and an infectious laugh, taking what could be called a laid-back approach to his future.

But some of his friends and associates sensed Robby did yearn for direction. Ronnie Rutkowski, 35, a 911 supervisor with the San Antonio police department, remembered sensing this. He befriended Robby when the boy was in junior high and became something of a mentor to him—teaching him to drive, and sharing heart-to-hearts.

Robby dropped out of high school, but hardly despaired. There were lakes and rivers around San Antonio that were waiting to be swum. There were football games to attend, and lots of parties.

While he was devoted to his friends, Robby was no follower. "He was actually very independent," said Rutkowski. "He did his own thing." This character trait proved crucial after Shannon was born in January 2001. When she arrived, Robby seemed to grow up overnight, which made everyone who knew him proud. Packing his high school equivalency degree, he began searching for work. He got a job as a waiter at IHOP, talked to Rutkowski about a future with the police force, but found nothing quickly with the benefits—the health insurance, the security—that he wanted for his daughter. The Army offered that, and, also, he would be following in the footsteps of his bygone father. "He wanted his daughter to be proud of him . . . He was a little scared, but excited," said his stepfather, Vincent Smith, of Robby's enlistment.

Robby was full of plans as he entered the service. Engaged to be married to Ana Perez of San Antonio, he had dreams—valid dreams, now—of building a family. Then, in May 2003, he was deployed to Iraq from Germany with his unit, Company B, First Battalion, 36th Infantry Regiment, First Armored Division.

In a June 15 letter to his mother he apologized for not writing more often, but explained that his 12-hour guard shifts and daily patrol duty left him little free time. He patrolled the Central Bank in Baghdad and the charred remains of one of Saddam Hussein's palaces, and thought about home.

On June 17, 2003, Robby was on duty at the bank when a grenade exploded nearby. He was fatally wounded at the age of 19.

Robby as a happy boy, a strapping youth and a doting dad. Opposite: In San Antonio, Robby's mother, Kim Smith, cradles Shannon as her husband looks on.

Dear Mom,

How are you doing? I am doing pretty good, even though it is hot as hell here . . .
It averages about 120° around noon time were I'm at right now. It really sucks because
it's not even summer time yet . . . Where I am at right now there is no life at all
. . . All you can see for miles is sand. The sand storms suck.

There's these spiders out here called camel spiders they're about as big as my
head. And there's black scorppions & theyre bodys are as big as my fist.

It's pretty funny. I go from doing drugs + partying all the time with my freinds
to making history all around the world. It's kinda cool, even though it is hot as . . .
Well tell everyone I miss them + love them very much, + I will see them as soon as I
can. I love you, mom. Bye.

Love always + forever,
Robby

* * * * *

Dear Mom,

Yesterday it was 130° outside. It feels like hell here. How is Shannon doing? Give
her big hugs + kisses for me. Make sure she knows her daddy loves her very much + I
will see her as soon as I can. I can't wait to get out of this place.

Someone shot at us last night. I was getting ready to go to sleep + I hear a pop-
pop and then the bullets ricocheted off the building, right outside the window I was
standing in front of . . . We've had random gunfire within a 100-meter radius all
night, every night, since I have been here. It kinda scares you the first couple of
nights, but you tend to get used to it.

It kinda sucks when all you can think about is there's someone out there trying to
kill you or your buddy next to you, and all you can do is hope you kill them first.

Love always + forever,
Robby

Shannon approaches her father's grave on the anniversary of his death. Right: Robby is memorialized in his mother's home.

Private Frantz's funeral took place on June 30, 2003, at San Antonio's Fort Sam Houston National Cemetery, where he was then buried. His mother accepted the Bronze Star and a Purple Heart on his behalf.

A year after his death, Frantz's mother, stepfather, sister and friends (including Rutkowski) returned to the cemetery to remember Robby. They talked about a curious legacy; Frantz's death had inspired some of his old buddies to go back and get their own high school equivalency degrees. Then they released balloons, and little Shannon freed two doves. One flew off, and the other, stunning everyone there, alit on Robby Frantz's headstone.

Pfc. Jesse Givens, Army

He was building a family—a loving wife, a happy young

stepson, another boy on the way—and, with the possible exception of defending his country, that is all he ever wanted to do. Nine days before Jesse A. Givens was killed, he wrote to his family: "I searched all my life for a dream and I found it in you."

Jesse was born in Springfield, Mo., on March 11, 1969 and grew up in a three-person household with his mother, Connie, and older brother, Reg. He was part American Indian on his mother's side, and proud of his heritage.

His father, Dennis, would sometimes take the boys fishing at Table Rock Lake, 50 miles south of the city, and the athletic Jesse would love to run through the woods. Even as a boy he wondered if he might one day be a soldier. But then he also loved to draw, especially the human form, and wondered if he might be an artist. He was always a mix of tough and tender: strong character, gentle nature. At Glendale High he played football and wrestled. He also painted and wrote poetry. He stuck up for kids who were being picked on. "He was usually quiet, and was often by himself," remembered Jennifer Moore-Davidson, Jesse's friend during high school. "But he was very loyal, and with his friends he would laugh a lot. His eyes would squint up, almost completely closing."

Still wondering where life might lead, Givens worked in the 1990s as a security officer at a local Sears, then at a ShopKo store in Joplin. There, in 1999, he struck up a relationship with Melissa Benfield, a single mom working one of the cash registers. They had little in common—she liked a party, he preferred a book—but there was evident chemistry. And, crucially, one-year-old Dakota, who had been cold to some other men that his mom had dated, adored Jesse—and the feeling was returned. "Dakota," Givens wrote from Iraq in 2003, "you are more son than I could ever ask for."

Jesse and Melissa moved in together. The ShopKo closed, and Jesse found a job as an ironworker. That was his place in life when, on September 11, 2001, he watched on television as the Twin Towers fell, and firemen, National Guardsmen—and, yes, ironworkers—leapt into the relief effort. "I should be there," he told Melissa. Instead, he decided to investigate that long-ago notion, and he enlisted in the Army.

He wondered whether, at age 32, he might struggle in boot camp. But he did fine, while enduring the taunts of "Grandpa" from his new colleagues.

Now things started to move very quickly. He and Melissa married on May 14, 2002. They settled in Colorado Springs, near Fort Carson, where Jesse was stationed with the Third Armored Cavalry Regiment. Even as the prospect of war with Iraq was becoming clear, the Givenses learned they were pregnant. They looked at the image on the sonogram, and the nickname came easily: "Bean."

By the time his 5,200-soldier regiment left for Iraq in April 2003, Jesse, while eager to serve his country, was uneasy. Suddenly, he had so much to lose. His dream had come true, but now he was heading into harm's way.

On May 1 Givens was driving an Abrams M1A2 tank toward fires that had been set by Iraqis near an ammo dump in Habbaniyah, west of Baghdad. When the heat became too much, Givens steered for higher ground, but a berm collapsed under the weight of the 70-ton tank, which plunged into a Euphrates River backwater. Givens, 34, drowned; his three-man crew escaped.

The three long letters of Jesse Givens, the first of which is excerpted on pages 69 and 70, are extraordinary in their message and intent. From the very moment he set foot in Iraq, Givens was filled with foreboding. He wrote the first of these letters to a beloved family that, he was sure, he would see no more. He instructed Melissa not to open it unless he died. The three letters all convey the same thoughts and emotions; in fact, the second and third were written simply as backups, in case the first didn't get through.

As Melissa has said, they were all goodbyes.

Jesse poses with Dakota and Melissa before departing for Iraq. Opposite: Melissa, Carson and Dakota at home in Colorado.

Second...

I don't know your name yet or even if a boy or girl. That does not mean... don't I love you too much. I know you are beautiful. I will always have with me the feeling of your body in your moms belly trying to move around. I used to lay by your mom while she slept and feel you kicking and rolling all night. I am so... I never got to see you or play with you. I... I am missing out on the most. I know you will grow to be a strong minded beautiful person. I...

Melissa,
Please only read if I don't come home. Please put it away and hopefully you will never have to read it.

My family:

I never thought that I would be writing a letter like this, I really don't know where to start. I've been getting bad feelings though and well if you are reading this.

I am forever in debt to you, Dakota, and the bean. I searched all my life for a dream and I found it in you. I would like to think that I made a positive difference in your lives. I will never be able to make up for the bad. I am so sorry. The happiest moments in my life all deal with my little family. I will always have with me the small moments we all shared. The moments when you quit taking life so serious and smiled. The sounds of a beautiful boys laughter or the simple nudge of a baby unborn. You will never know how complete you have made me. Each one of you. You saved me from lonliness and taught me how to think beyond myself. You taught me how to live and to love. You opened my eyes to a world I never dreamed existed. I am proud of you. Stay on the path you chose. Never lose sight of what is important.

Dakota you are more son than I could ever ask for. I can only hope I was half the dad. I used to be your "danny" but, no matter what it makes me proud that you chose me. You taught me how to care until it hurts, you taught me how to smile again. You taught me that life isn't so serious and sometimes you have to play. You have a big beautiful heart. Through life you need to keep it open and follow it. Never be afraid to be yourself. I will always be there in our park when you dream so we can still play. I hope someday you will have a son like mine. Make them smile and shine just like you. I love you Toad. I hope someday you will understand why I didn't come home. Please be proud of me. Please don't stop loving life. Take in every breath like its your first. I love you Toad, I will always be there with you. I'll be in the sun, shadows, dreams, and joys of your life.

Bean, I never got to see you but I know in my heart you are beautiful. I know you will be strong and big hearted just like your mom and brother. I will always have with me the feel of the soft nudges on your moms belly, and the joy I felt when we found out you were on your way. I dream of you every night, I will always. Don't ever think that since I wasn't around that I didn't love you. You were conceived of love and I came to this terrible place for love. I love you as I do your mom and brother with all my heart and soul. Please understand that I had to be gone so that I could take care of my family. I love you Bean ... [letter continued on next page]

I have never been so blessed as I was the day I met Melissa Dawn Benfield. You are my Angel, soulmate, wife, lover, and best friend. I am sorry. I did not want to have to write this letter. There is so much more I need to say, so much more I need to share. A lifetimes worth. I married you for a million lifetimes. That's how long I will be with you . . . Do me a favor. After you tuck Toad and Bean in, give them hugs and kisses from me. Go outside look at the stars and count them. Don't forget to smile.

Love Always
Your husband
Jess

From his journal:

I am not going to pretend that I understand why we are thinking of going to war with Iraq. I know the reasons we are given—some seem more credible than others.

No matter what, I will go, and fight with all my heart. Not to win a war but to come home to my wife and children.

I took an oath to protect my country, not for the sake of saving the world but for the hopes that my family wouldn't have to live in a world filled with hate, fear and sadness, a world to which America was exposed to on September 11, 2001. I just ask that we do things for the right reasons. I ask that you understand that when you send soldiers into battle that they are not just numbers. I ask that you see our roles as fathers, sons, daughters, wives and husbands, as well as seeing us proud Americans who want to serve our country.

When all is said and done, will we, the United States military, shed blood or pass at the hands of our enemy for a just cause? Will you remember those who we leave behind and honor them as well as our fallen brothers and sisters?

Jesse Givens

PEKOL
THOMAS A SR
SP4   USA
938   2003

RED HUSBAND
PS GRANDPA

GIVENS
JESSE ALAN
PFC   USA
IRAQI FREEDOM
BSM PH ARCOM
1969 . 2003
TO THY OWN SELF
BE TRUE

KELLBARTH
JOHN J
TEC 4   USA
WORLD WAR II

RAUHO
JAMES ANT
SR   US
1956   20

BELOVED HU
FATHER AN

SMIT
DANN
L CPL
VIETN

Opposite: Melissa, wearing Jesse's dog tags. Above: Carson, at his father's vault.

Throughout May 2003, 27-year-old Melissa Givens had constant reminders of her husband—friends' condolences, the funeral, letters from Jesse that arrived posthumously, the letters that she had written to him that never got through, and now were being returned. On May 14, which would have been their first wedding anniversary, she received flowers and a card from Jesse. And on May 29, four weeks after his father had been killed in Iraq, Carson Givens, theretofore known as "Bean," was born in Colorado.

S. Sgt. Stephen Hattamer, Army

If the military gave silver watches as well as

Silver Stars, Stephen Hattamer would have earned his. Fresh into the Marine Corps reserves at 18, he was, in 2003, an Army reservist finally enjoying the rhythms of civilian life with his family. Stephen's fulfilling career in the two branches, which included a long stint in the active Army, had taken him to many places around the world. But now a more tranquil scene in Gwinn, Mich.—working in telecommunications on the former K.I. Sawyer Air Force Base—seemed just fine. Stephen, his wife, Karen, and their children (teenagers Bryce and Alyssa and 12-year-old Tyler) were settling down. Hattamer was even thinking of returning to school, perhaps to pursue a career in medicine.

The things that interested Hattamer in those days before the war included his family, his faith, his fitness—he biked, lifted weights and skied—always in communion with his fellow man. An elder at Victory Lutheran Church, he was a ready volunteer to drive the Sunday school bus or to mentor troubled kids. When a fire ravaged a local woman's house, Hattamer was there in an instant, helping cart debris, rebuild and repaint. With the Air Force base shifting to nonmilitary use, there was a plague of unemployment in the area. One neighboring family was so destitute they couldn't even afford to relocate when circumstances dictated that they must. Hattamer corralled a friend to help, loaded the family's possessions into his truck and got the job done.

He had a reputation as a good Samaritan and, by the by, as a pretty mean baker. He was adept at executing his mom's recipe for German chocolate cake, which made an appearance at all Hattamer kids' birthday parties (not to mention Dad's own). When a friend needed to talk after September 11, Hattamer rushed over—but not before whipping up some brownies: good comfort food.

Hattamer saw the war with Iraq looming and suspected his quiet life was coming to an end. He was right. Stephen's unit, the 652nd Engineer Battalion, U.S. Army Reserve, was deployed in April of 2003.

As he had been in Gwinn, Hattamer was all about action and outreach in Iraq. His team's job was to build bridges, but when work was done he would be off visiting with Iraqi families, getting to know about the country and culture. For his colleagues in the service, he started a Bible study group, and became known as a useful counselor for soldiers suffering anger or depression. He phoned home often and wrote letters. In order to encourage his kids to write back, he included self-addressed envelopes.

In a 2003 letter written as the holidays approached, he asked for a care package of coffee for Christmas. On the 25th of December, Hattamer was killed when his living quarters came under mortar attack in the city of Baquba in the eastern part of Iraq. Stephen C. Hattamer was 43.

Dad, on his 40th birthday, blows out the candles on a cake of his own making. Opposite: Tyler and Alyssa flank their mother, Karen, at home in Gwinn. (Bryce was away at college on this occasion.)

Good morning Karen and children,

Well, one more week down and 25 more weeks to be here. The memorial for SFC Gabriel-son . . . was today. He has a wife and 2 daughters and a boy the youngest of all three being 15.

We are not suppose to get into any other . . . battles but the Iraqis are ambush-ing us on routes and making things real difficult for us and them. I cannot under-stand why our government really thinks they can change their behavior . . . They tear down what we build and steal it or take it to the pawn shop because they have no jobs.

Well, I know these last two letters were not very up beat but I have had a real crappy week, from us losing a soldier to the Iraqis not caring. I'm real ready to come home.

God Bless!

* * * * *

Hello Karen,

Happy Anniversary to you! . . . I still can't believe that we made it to 20 years. Well I suppose you already heard that we got extended and all the way till spring. Man I tell ya they really have their head up their butts on this one.

I have to admit though the colonel has practiced a better speech. The first one he basically called us a schmuck but now he contends, he needs to complete the missions. He says he needs boots on the ground. I really do not know if I'll even be able to see Bryce graduate.

Well we have finally come to the point of the deployment when we don't look for security but uniform violations. Not having your chin strap on . . . boots not tied, helmet not on, t-shirts not tucked in.

Boy the nights are cooling below 70 and I only have the little blanket and got a little cold . . . I really need me a snuggle bunnie to cuddle, but I think I was nev-er issued one. Well, Happy Anniversary. Hey, I was thinking for Christmas, you could send me some coffee—French Vanilla or Hazelnut.

Well, happy anniversary
God Bless
Stephen

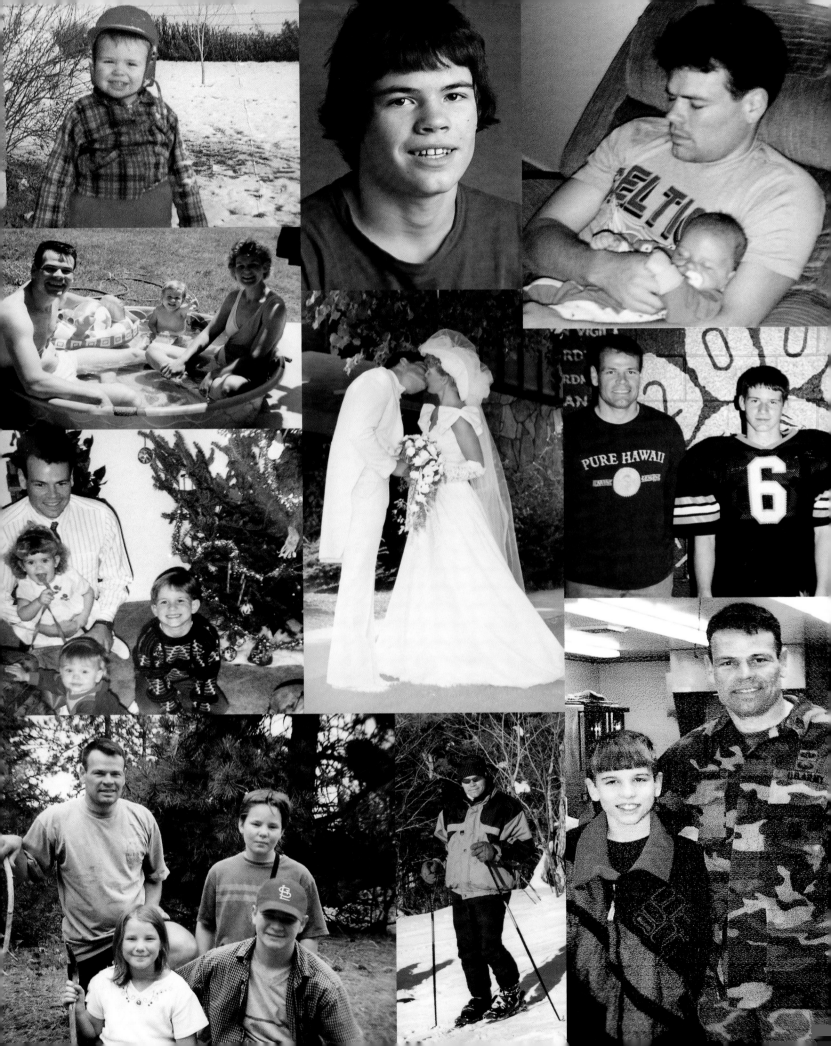

Hello Alyssa!

How are you doing honey? Is everything going well over there? I hope so. I miss getting letters from you guys, so here are a couple of envelopes. Have you started cheerleading for the Basketball season . . . I could just hear you saying, Shake your booty and Stomp-em, Gwinn, Stomp-em!

Well, I hope you have a good Thanksgiving and I hope you are not eating too much candy. I am very proud of you, Alyssa.

I Love You,
Miss ya too!
Daddy

Hello Tyler!

How are you? What's up? Howz school! I miss you buddy.

Did you have fun doing football with Bryce. Pretty cool, I never got to do that with my brothers. They always would beat me up or something. Is school work hard this year or have you found a study partner?

Tyler, I sure would like to receive a letter from you, I went ahead and sent you some envelopes so all you have to do is just put a stamp on the envelope.

I miss you alot,
Dad

Hello Squeeker, how is Alyssa? I hope [...] through and that you [...] classes. I also [...] having good Teachers

Well I have to [...] Christmas still at le[ast] hope you all will [...] [...] with these days.

[Wel]l I really miss you, [...] [a]nd your Something mo[re]. sending it home soo[n]

I love you Alyssa.

Hello Alyssa, I wrote you a poem too. I love you dearly honey

Hello my Alyssa
how is it going
I really miss ya
hope things are not boring
you know I want to hug ya
can you hear Ty snoring
you know I love ya
are you still growing
I have something for ya
No matter where your going
Take it with ya
    Faith-Hope-Love

I love you too! even in Iraq!

        Love,
        Daddy

Hello Karen, I'm having such a [...] time with email that I figure I'll go with ole reliable. Now we hear [...] all the mail will go to Kuwait [...] they truck it up to Bagdad [...] back south to us. So, bott[om] line the mail is going to rea[lly] suck now too! Its like a ra[sh] that won't go away and keeps flarin[g] Anyway, everything is going to tak[e] longer to leave and to come here [...] [lik]e 2 days to find mail [pack]ages. I have 37 more [...] [to] go and so far its j[ust] [...] got your email on that [...] I'm very thankful [...] [...] put it in his regi[on] [...] make us get together a[...] [bod]ies life side by side [...] and toe to toe head [...] [of] course book to book [...] [no]t so lonesome over [...] [...], but I pray that [...] [...] get together when [...] [...] emailed Bryce and he [...] twice already. He [...] [...] and like there is n[...] [...] step. I pray tha[t...] [...] to go to church. [...] [...] you Karen Hattamer [...] [...] with the good Lord [...] [...] day soon we will be [...] [...] very good job so far [...] [...] knowing whats going [...]

Opposite: Hattamer's uniforms and other clothing were shipped home to Gwinn in trunks.
Above: In Iraq on Christmas Day, 2003.

Staff Sergeant Hattamer's funeral was held on January 2, 2004 at Victory Lutheran Church in Gwinn. The service there, and a subsequent full military ceremony at Christ Lutheran Church in Spokane, Wash., where Hattamer grew up, were presided over by Mark Sippola, the late soldier's pastor and best friend. Sippola read an e-mail message that Steve had sent to Karen on the day he was killed. It said, "I know that with faith, hope and love we will be alright."

Pfc. Raheen Heighter, Army

He knew what he wanted to do with his life: go to college, go into business for himself and then take care of his mother, Cathy, whom he called in a letter written just a month before he died, "the most important person in my life." But the plan needed work. Raheen Heighter knew that his family couldn't afford to send him to college. One avenue seemed to be the Army— a smart move that would enable him to serve his country while getting invaluable experience as well as that much-needed financial aid for school.

His mother appreciated Raheen's dream, but tried to be a wise counsel. A hairdresser with her own salon, Beyond Images of Beauty, in Bay Shore, N.Y., she knew only too well the rigors of building a business. She told her go-getter son, "Life just doesn't happen like that. Success is a process."

Deeply impressed by Raheen's artistic ability, she believed that he should, perhaps, pursue a career as an artist. Her efforts to inspire him were energetic. When he was 14, Raheen picked up a pencil and executed an intricate, powerful study in blue of a strongly built father cradling a young boy. Cathy was so moved that she had the portrait reproduced by a friend and displayed it in her shop. The original she hung at home.

Cathy was equally vigorous about keeping both of her boys on the straight and narrow. In school, Raheen was a good kid, thanks largely to his mother. On one occasion, in junior high school, he got into some minor trouble. Cathy, when informed of this, not only showed up at the school but trailed her son to every class—even to the cafeteria—to emphasize how deeply she cared about his behavior. "That was the quietest lunch period we'd ever had, because children don't want to mess with someone's mother," one of Raheen's eighth-grade teachers, Betty Greene, remembered to the Long Island newspaper *Newsday*. "And after that, there were no more problems with Raheen."

As he grew, Raheen proved as proactive as his mother. He showed his work in local art fairs. He became a video game phenom, mastering each as fast as he could, then reselling it in the neighborhood. When he wasn't vanquishing video games, he'd devour self-help books. "His brain was always working," his older brother, Glynn, told *Newsday*. Heighter went out for football at Brentwood High and made the varsity team. He was achieving in several realms and continued to harbor that idea of joining the Army to get ahead. Still a high schooler, he tried to enlist, but when a recruitment officer approached his mother for her permission, she said, "Don't even ask. Get out of here."

Raheen graduated from Brentwood in 2000 and worked for a year in a brokerage firm. He began studying for a licensing exam, but, characteristically, found himself in a hurry for the next chapter. When he was old enough to enlist without his mother's consent, he did just that. He walked into her salon on August 7, 2001, and told her that he'd joined the Army. Loaded down with three duffel bags, he left the next day.

Assigned to the 101st Airborne Division based out of Fort Campbell, Ky., the kid who'd never been farther away from home than Disney World was shipped to Korea for a year's tour of duty. Shortly after he returned home, he was redeployed to Iraq in February of 2003. With his eye on the greater prize of a successful post-Army life, Raheen tried to keep his head down and do his job.

After an initial period of intense fighting in and around Baghdad, Raheen felt that things had calmed down. He sent reassuring messages home and was optimistic that he would return; it was just a matter of time. But early in the morning of July 24, 2003, insurgents ambushed his convoy en route to the city of Qayyarah, north of Baghdad. Attacking with gunfire and rocket-propelled grenades, they killed three, including Raheen Heighter, age 22.

As he told his family before he died, he felt that Iraq had changed him, improved him and better prepared him to fulfill his lifelong dreams.

Young Raheen was his mother's dance partner, and, at right, a gridiron standout. Opposite: Cathy Heighter and her son, Glynn, at home.

Dear Mother,

We have totally abdicated Saddam from power and now we are in the liberalization process. I'm eating good, working out, and reading good literature, now that the war is over . . . The group of soldiers I'm working with now are good people. They take care of me and I take care of them. Tell everybody I said, Hey.

Love,
Raheen

* * * * *

Dear Mother,

Today is a blissful day. Mother, you are the most important person in my life and today is the first time I realized you (only) have tried your hardest to bring the bestowed, hidden, optimistic and spontaneous qualities out of me . . . Well, Mother, my feet have been placed on the firm ground. Without your teaching me what you have it would not have been possible. As I sit here in tears, I thank you.

Time goes by like a continuous groundhog day over here. In the beginning there was a lot of blood shed, but now it's all over. Though there still are some terrorist that don't wan't us here. The good news is I will be home to see you in september, or october the latest.

Love
Raheen

* * * * *

Dear Mother

The war is not over. The last letter I sent you was misleading, although we thought our duty here was almost over. To let you know Im doing fine. Time drags by, but I try to stay busy. My duty over here for the past couple weeks have been that of a police officer. There has always been a threat of violence towrds us US soldiers. Now were looking at being home no latter than december. Tell everyone I said hi.

Love
Raheen

PFC Heighter
A-1 327 InF (Fot)
Unit 96018
APO AE 09325-6018

Carrie Adams and Ann Stevens

Bashore N.Y
11706

BY AIR MAIL

5 27 03

Dear Grandma and Aunt Ann

How are yall doing? Me myself Im
in the shade writing a letter. Thank
you grandma for the picture. Though
I need a picture of of Anne Oakley
to. Aunt Ann tell Melivin I said
Hi. I miss yall all more now than
ever before in my life. I can't
wait to get home to taste a sweet
potato pie, and taste some of Anns
Kollet Greens. Ann if I never
told you I love you I do, and Grandma
you are my one of my mentors.

In Bay Shore there was a two-day wake and more than 1,000 people gathered in and around Rose's Funeral Home for Raheen Tyson Heighter's service. Heighter was posthumously awarded a Purple Heart and the Bronze Star. Further honoring him, the northeast corner of Pine Aire Drive and Fifth Avenue in Bay Shore was renamed Raheen Heighter Drive.

Cathy Heighter continues to keep the memory of her son alive, with his artwork prominently displayed on the walls of her home and salon.

Pfc. Francisco Martinez-Flores, Marines

He gave his life for his country

even before it was, fully and officially, his country. The backstory: Samuel Martinez and Martha Flores fell in love and married in Mexico, began a family, then followed the immigrants' dream and headed for America. Leaving their native land, they settled in Duarte, near Los Angeles, where they raised their two girls and two boys. Francisco, their oldest, was something of a joker, and built a large circle of friends at Maxwell Elementary School in Duarte, and then at Duarte High, where he also played football. On off-season weekends, Francisco would hang with his buddies, or work on his '54 Ford with his dad.

That was his life when he graduated in the spring of 2000 and decided on the next step.

To Martinez-Flores, the Marines represented a road to an education that he could not otherwise afford. And if he wanted to be a police detective or stockbroker one day, as he professed, then he needed an education. He enlisted, survived basic training and was assigned to the First Tank Battalion, First Marine Division, Marine Corps Air-Ground Combat Center at the serenely named Twentynine Palms base in California. He matured in the Marines—the Corps steadied him—but he never lost his carefree side. When he was stationed in Kuwait, he took to collecting exotic, sometimes dangerous desert animals—a sidewinder snake, a scorpion, a lizard he named Mr. Biggles—and keeping them in empty ammo canisters. Once, when his Charlie Company unit passed the tanks of Delta Company, Martinez-Flores mooned his friendly rivals.

From the get-go, nothing went smoothly for the First Tank Battalion Marines in Iraq. Shortly after moving out of Kuwait, they came upon what they thought were Iraqi citizens. Instead, it was an ambush by soldiers loyal to Saddam, traveling in disguise. Then, late on Monday, March 24, 2003, they reached the Euphrates River, which they needed to cross, only to learn from Marines camped nearby that the bridge was unfinished and perhaps impassable. Debate continued for an hour as the night grew darker, then the column was ordered to proceed along a different route. It did so in eerie, hazy moonlight. The tanks rumbled down an embankment, across a dry marsh, skirting a bend in the river so that they could continue on course. When the spectral night was over, the tank carrying Martinez-Flores and three other Marines was missing. Others in the battalion, trying to figure out what may have happened to the missing tank, wondered if the driver had been shot, or if he had simply become disoriented. No one knew for sure as the dawn slowly crept over the desert, but most suspected that the vehicle was at the bottom of the river.

Before he died, Francisco, 21, had written to his girlfriend, Marisela Campos, and to his mother. Those letters follow.

Francisco, the smiling boy, grows up to be an all-business Marine. Opposite, from left: Francisco's sister Marleen, mother Martha, sister Nayeli, father Samuel and kid brother Sammy at home in Duarte, Calif.

My dearest Princess,

Hi, sweetie. How are you I'm alright A little nervous. By this time you probably know whats going on. I Love You, Sweetie. We are already in our attack positions. So please just pray for me. I Love you. I'll see you sooner than you think. Its a short letter, but I dont have that much time. I'll pray every night And I'll wear your rosary. I Love You. Please take care. Hope to hear from you soon.

Sorry for the sloppy writing. Love you, sweetie. Look up at the sky and smile when you get this.

Love Always,
Francisco

Dear Mom,

I hope this finds you well. I am writing to tell you I'm fine.

I think you all know what is happening, and I hope you are praying for me. I love you very much. God will reward me in the future for the sacrifice I am making. Take care, and I hope to see you in the next few months.

Sincerely, your son, who loves you very much,
Francisco

In the days immediately following the midnight incident by the river, a vicious sand-storm made a search impossible. The mystery of what had happened to the tank carrying Martinez-Flores and his three fellow Marines lasted for several days, and then on March 28, 2003, Navy divers learned the worst: that the tank was upside down at the bottom of the Euphrates, 20 feet under water, and the four inside had drowned.

Unique circumstances attended two of the victims. Lance Corporal Patrick O'Day of Santa Rosa, Calif., had been born in Scotland, and, of course, Martinez-Flores was a native of Mexico. Neither had yet attained U.S. citizenship, though Martinez-Flores's paperwork was in the system. They were, at the time, among approximately 31,000 "green card" servicemen and women defending the United States.

After having been killed fighting for what he considered to be his country, Martinez-Flores was granted posthumous citizenship, and the post office in Duarte was named in his honor.

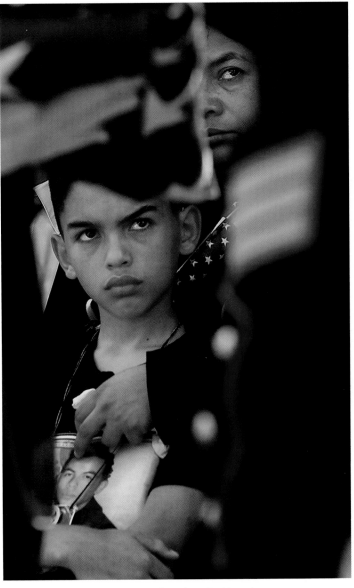

Francisco's brother Sammy and mother Martha at the funeral service in Monrovia, Calif.

Spc. Holly McGeogh, Army

It's not every high schooler who knows for a certainty that the military's for her, but Holly McGeogh, an effervescent and confident teen, was not your usual high schooler. At Truman High in the Detroit suburb of Taylor, she acted on her conviction, joining the Junior Reserve Officers' Training Corps, where she proved herself a leader. She would not hesitate to raise her voice to keep her colleagues in line, and then would disarm them with her sense of humor. "Holly was a mentor to me," said Sara Zaucha, a classmate who credits Holly with spurring her along in the JROTC program. "I was shy and quiet before I met Holly, and she'd yell at me to be louder. She was the kind who would talk to everyone; she didn't care if you were popular or unpopular. She was a good teacher and helpful if you were having a problem. She was always there for you." McGeogh was pure energy, and the collection of medals on her JROTC uniform grew week after week.

She enlisted immediately upon graduating from Truman, and pulled assignment with Company A, Fourth Forward Support Battalion, Fourth Infantry Division out of Fort Hood, Tex. In Iraq she served as a light truck mechanic. She was close to danger throughout her tour. In October 2003, a woman in her division was killed outside the gates of Saddam Hussein's palace in Tikrit. Holly's mother, Paula, younger brother, Robert, and stepfather, Michael Zasadny, suffered for two days, knowing a female soldier from Holly's unit had died but not knowing which one. Paula leaned on some friends that she had made in the Michigan Military Moms support group. Finally, Holly got through to her and let her know that, in fact, it had been her roommate who had been killed. If she didn't return from Iraq, she told her family, please know that she felt she had died for a reason.

On January 31, 2004, Holly was traveling in a convoy in Kirkuk, a major oil-producing area some 60 miles north of Tikrit. Suddenly, a homemade bomb exploded, killing McGeogh along with Sergeant Eliu Miersandoval of California and Corporal Juan Cabralbanuelos of Kansas. McGeogh was 19.

During her time in Iraq, she stayed in touch with folks in Michigan whenever she could—by phone, letter and e-mail.

In one haunting e-mail message, she talks of her embarrassment at being overly cautious with a suspected IED—an Improvised Explosive Device—which is precisely the kind of bomb that finally took her life.

The mechanic works a shift in Iraq. Opposite: Holly's younger brother Robert, stepfather Michael and mom Paula in Troy, Mich.

During her first Christmas away from home, McGeogh, front and center, poses with friends and a guy named Santa.

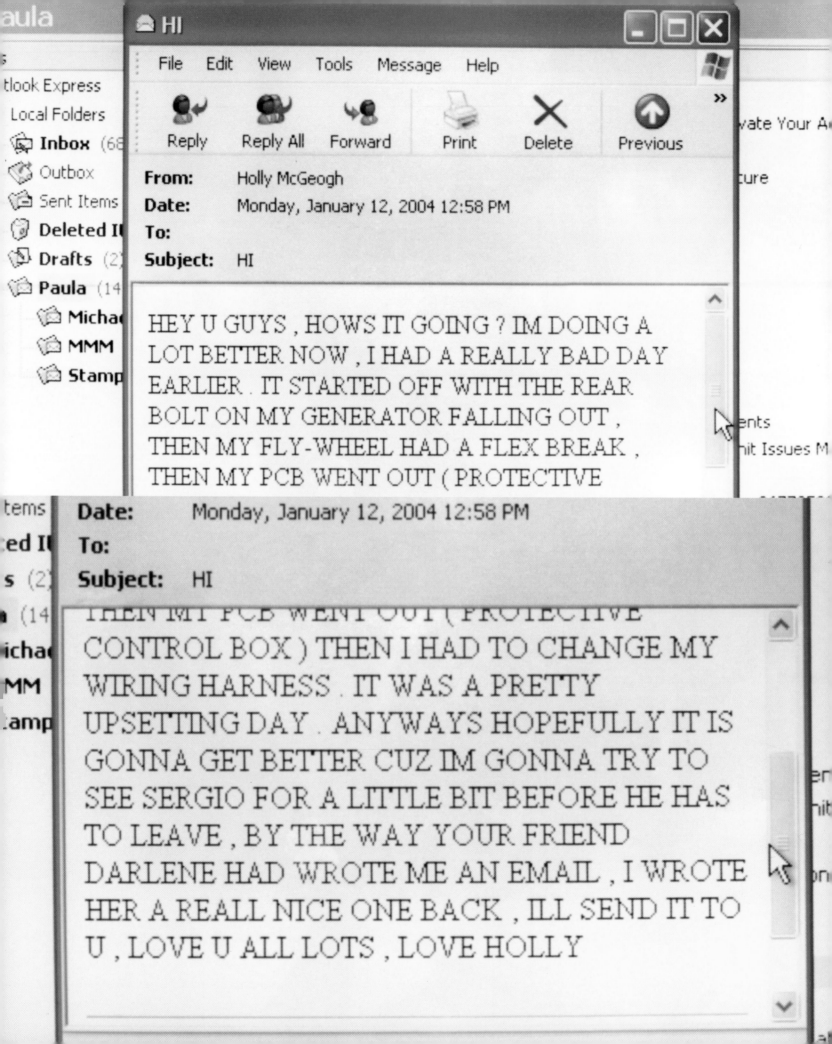

HI

File Edit View Tools Message Help

Reply Reply All Forward Print Delete Previous

From: Holly McGeogh
Date: Monday, January 12, 2004 12:58 PM
To:
Subject: HI

HEY U GUYS , HOWS IT GOING ? IM DOING A
LOT BETTER NOW , I HAD A REALLY BAD DAY
EARLIER . IT STARTED OFF WITH THE REAR
BOLT ON MY GENERATOR FALLING OUT ,
THEN MY FLY-WHEEL HAD A FLEX BREAK ,
THEN MY PCB WENT OUT (PROTECTIVE

Date: Monday, January 12, 2004 12:58 PM
To:
Subject: HI

THEN MY PCB WENT OUT (PROTECTIVE
CONTROL BOX) THEN I HAD TO CHANGE MY
WIRING HARNESS . IT WAS A PRETTY
UPSETTING DAY . ANYWAYS HOPEFULLY IT IS
GONNA GET BETTER CUZ IM GONNA TRY TO
SEE SERGIO FOR A LITTLE BIT BEFORE HE HAS
TO LEAVE , BY THE WAY YOUR FRIEND
DARLENE HAD WROTE ME AN EMAIL , I WROTE
HER A REALL NICE ONE BACK , ILL SEND IT TO
U , LOVE U ALL LOTS , LOVE HOLLY

HI U GUYS,

WHATS GOING ON ON THAT SIDE OF THE WORLD? THINGS ARE OK OVER HERE. TODAY WHEN MY SECTION ROLLED OUT OF THE GATE WE HAD SEEN SOMEONE DROP A CAN ON THE GROUND AND WE THOUGHT IT WAS AN IED [IMPROVISED EXPLOSIVE DEVICE]. SO I STOPPED RITE AWAY AND BACKED UP, THE OTHER 2 VEHICLES HAD ALREADY WENT BY IT. WE GOT OUT AND PULLED SECURITY. THEN WE CALLED CHARLIE COMPANY OUT TO TAKE A LOOK AT IT. WELL, IT ENDED UP NOT BEING AN IED, I HAD FELT A LITTLE EMBARRESSED, BUT AT THE SAME TIME I KNEW THAT WE HAD DONE THE RITE THING. AND I HAVE FULL CONFIDENCE IN THE PEOPLE THAT I WORK WITH THAT IF THEY FELT IF ANYBODYS LIFE WAS IN DANGER THAT THEY WOULD DO EVERYTHING IN THEIR POWER TO NOT LET ANYTHING HAPPEN. I KNOW THAT I WOULD DO IT FOR THEM, IN A HEART BEAT.

I REALLY MISS U ALL SOOOOOO MUCH, TO BE HONEST IF IT WASNT FOR U GUYS, I WOULD HAVE NEVER BEEN ABLE TO MAKE IT THROUGH ALL THIS.

I MISS U GUYS SO MUCH AND LOVE U GUYS WITH ALL MY HEART,

LOVE HOLLY

* * * * *

Mom,

Hey, momma. Just want to say that I hope you do have a good Christmas and a Happy New Year. I know it won't be the same. It's gonna be different for me, too — My first Christmas ever by myself. I gotta be strong and so do you.

So please put on the Santa hat and have some fun. If you decide to get drunk, drink some Captain Morgan's Spiced Rum and some Dr. Pepper for me — K?

Remember when I get back we're gonna go shopping and get pampered. A whole week together. And you're not gonna need those pills anymore, so we can throw them out—K?

But anyways, I love you with all my heart and I couldn't ask for a better mom, 'cuz I got the best one in the world already! Have a Merry Christmas and a Happy New Year!

Love you with all my heart,
Holly

On February 9, 2004, an honor guard bears McGeogh to her rest. Opposite: The family truck now carries a memorial.

Holly McGeogh was the first Michigan servicewoman to be killed in Operation Iraqi Freedom. Back home, she was remembered for her vivacity and dedication to task. At the funeral service at St. Joseph's Roman Catholic Church in Wyandotte, members and alumni of Truman's JROTC program filled the pews. "She died for something she believed in," said the Reverend T.J. Moloney. He added: "Her death reminds us that freedom is not free."

McGeogh was posthumously promoted to Specialist, and awarded a Purple Heart and the Bronze Star.

Capt. Pierre Piché, Army

In the 1970s, northern Vermont looked like refuge and salvation to Lisa, a single mother from New York City who was looking for a new life for herself and her only child, Pierre. They started in Colchester, and at age six, Pierre gained a stepfather when Lisa married Hugh Johnson. The family moved to South Hero and then, when Pierre was 14, to Starksboro, a town whose name does it no justice. It is a serene village in the foothills of the Green Mountains, a place of historic houses on the main street and, on the outskirts, streams and ponds and waterfalls.

The outdoors of Vermont informed the boy. He played on and around the dam on the Winooski River; he attended Camp Bear Paw in Bolton Valley in the summer. He developed into a loving and happy kid. His middle name, Esprit, was apt; with flair, if not flamboyance, he shouted his French Canadian heritage with a trademark beret that he wore even in his youth. In his later teens, Pierre and his friends would drive in his Ford Taurus to shooting ranges nearby, where they would blast away.

There was a quieter, contemplative side to Pierre as well. To a reporter from the *Chicago Tribune,* Lisa Johnson remembered her son as a lifelong romantic and "someone who was a reader, a pianist, someone who was complex." He enjoyed Beethoven, she said, and discussed Spinoza with her when he was six. He was influenced and inspired by his teachers, and voiced an aspiration to teach, himself, one day.

Despite Pierre's affinity for guns, many who knew him were surprised, and his mother was heartbroken, when he signed up for Army ROTC in college. His career in the service was distinguished as he rose through the ranks in the 101st Airborne Division. He fell in love with a woman from Illinois named Cherish, and they married in 1999 in a full military ceremony, complete with a canopy of crossed swords for the couple to walk beneath. They made their home near Fort Campbell in Kentucky. When Pierre learned in early 2003 that he was to be deployed to Iraq, he went about the house sticking Post-it notes with love messages on every available surface.

In Iraq, Piché stayed in constant touch with those back home, sending e-mail messages and photos. Many of the pictures were of him with abandoned animals that he adopted and fed. In one letter, Piché confided to his mother his plans to leave the military once he got back home, which he expected to be in February of 2004. "I am proud to defend my country," he wrote on August 6, 2003, "but I don't want to be defending it constantly for the next 10-15 years."

His assignment in Iraq was to serve as a maintenance officer—essentially a desk job. He joked with his wife that the only way he'd earn a Purple Heart would be to develop carpal tunnel syndrome. But, of course, wars are filled with stories of ill fate. In November, Piché was due for a leave, and was told to take it even though he was reluctant to do so. On November 15, 2003, he was traveling on one of two U.S. Black Hawk helicopters that collided in the air over Mosul. Piché and 16 soldiers were killed in the crash.

On the following pages are messages from a man who, at 29, was finishing the military part of his life, during which he served honorably and well, and was looking forward to the future.

The prodigious Pierre brushes up on his Beethoven, circa 1980. Opposite page: Lisa and Hugh in Vermont.

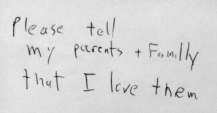

Please tell
my parents + family
that I love them

Hi, baby girl,

I miss you like crazy, darling. I do not like being so far away from you and not being able to live our life . . . It kills me that we ever wasted one day fighting or otherwise being miserable . . . I hope that time will start passing more quickly, but right now it is dragging.

It is hard to even imagine 6 months right now but we must take this one day at a time—like baby steps. Years from now, this will just be one of the many chapters in our lives. I think we will remember how much it sucked but we will also remember the lessons it taught us. We will be stronger for having survived this. Every day and every moment from the time I come home is going to be precious.

I am really looking forward to a nice, boring life with my sweet wife . . . I <u>swear</u> I will make it home to you. I put up all the "post it" notes so no matter where you look—you will see a piece of me. I love you. I will see you later.

No good-byes,
Pierre

Hi, Mom and Hugh,

Greetings from Iraq. I just wanted to write you a letter to let you know that I am fine and am thinking about you.

Also, I wanted to thank you for the package. Everybody looks at me like I'm crazy when I drink straight maple syrup but I tell them I am a Vermonter and the taste reminds me of fall in Vermont.

The Iraqi military isn't much of a threat, but I was worried about angry civilians/terrorists/suicide bombers who wanted to kill the "Yankee Devil." I am sure there are some of these maniacs out there but most of the people seem very glad to see us. People are always trying to give us gifts (goats, bread, etc) to say Thank You for getting rid of Saddam. People show us their scars from the Iraqi torture chambers and tell us about their relatives who have been taken away, never to be seen again. I know we cannot entirely change this hell hole, but maybe being here will make things a little better.

Love,
Pierre

* * * * *

Hi Mom and Hugh,

I guess I will be here longer than the 6 months we originally planned on. Nobody is happy about it . . . I am definitely looking forward to being out of the military. It was good for what it did for me, I don't regret it, but it is time to go . . . It is easy to do the math. The US currently has substantial forces in Kosovo, Afghanistan, Sianni Egypt, Korea and of course, Iraq . . . That adds up to 5 major deployments, not to mention . . . the next crisis that is just on the horizon. The army only has 10 divisions so troops will either be ramping up for deployment, deployed or just returning from a deployment for the next 5 to 10 years at least. I am proud to defend my country, but I don't want to be defending it constantly for the next 10-15 years . . . I want to . . . have something resembling a personal/ home life . . . I want to . . . have time to do all the things I have missed out for all these years . . . I miss you and love you very much. I hate the idea of missing out on the holidays once again. Hopefully this will be the last year for that.

Pierre

At the Mountain View Chapel in Essex Junction, Vt., soldiers wait to attend the casket of Captain Piché.

In November 2003, Cherish Piché prepared to travel to Vermont for her late husband's funeral. Putting on her coat, she found two last Post-it notes in the pockets. "We will always be together," read one, and the other: "I will always love you!"

Pierre Piché's body was cremated. His ashes are in three places. Cherish placed some on a wooded trail near Nashville where the couple liked to walk, and in the ocean off Florida, another place they loved. And in Vermont, a group of Pierre's friends and relations, including his mother, drove to a pond where Pierre had played as a child, and scattered his ashes on the water.

Lisa also keeps some in a small locket that she wears on a necklace.

Spc. Robert Wise, Army

No one could miss the smile.

Robert's father, David, told the *Tallahassee Democrat* that his boy could "reel you in with a smile that was all teeth." Other friends and relatives affectionately recalled it as being "goofy." Born in Key West, Florida, in 1982, young Robert was as sunny as the island paradise where he spent his early years. The second child of David and Tammy, Robert was a fun-loving kid who acted in school plays, was an enthusiastic trouper in a local children's circus and avidly devoured fantasies of all kinds. He was devoted to Superman, his all-time favorite movie was *The Wizard of Oz* and, it is fair to say, he was a lifelong *Star Trek* nut. Amidst the news that he sent home to his mother from Iraq were critiques of the latest novels in the *Trek* series that he read during downtime in the desert.

After his parents divorced, Robert and his mother moved north to Tallahassee. There, he quickly made his mark at his new school, Amos P. Godby High, where he ran cross-country and played soccer. It was also at Godby that Robert began to exhibit a contrasting side to the cheerful boy who loved to drift into fantastic realms. He signed up for Air Force Junior ROTC, a hard-core and fiercely realistic endeavor. Robert's serious streak and feelings of social responsibility were encapsulated in a favorite passage of his from Daniel Webster: "God grants liberty only to those who love it, and are always ready to defend it."

Robert proved to be a natural leader, a young man who set an example of high standards for himself and those around him. "Robert was selected as a Cadets' Corps Commander," said Senior Master Sergeant Stephen C. Sullivan, who taught Wise in Junior ROTC and also in an aerospace science class. "That doesn't happen to everybody. Our program's emphasis is on community service, helping the March of Dimes, working to keep Leon County clean. If we needed people somewhere at 6:30, Robert would be there at 5:30. And I'm talking about the morning. If the program was over at one, he'd stay to help any way he could until three or four. No job was too small or too dirty. He'd just do it. He was the kind of person who gave 180 percent to everything he did."

When he turned 17, Robert was determined to sign up to serve in the Florida National Guard, but needed his mother's signature on the papers. She was hesitant. But when she discussed it with him, he said, "I know where I'm going and I know how I'm going to get there." On hearing the strength of his conviction, she gave in and signed the paper. He completed boot camp in August 2000 and was assigned to the Third Battalion, 124th Regiment, 53rd Infantry Brigade. While a Guardsman, Robert continued to work at a local electric supply company and enrolled in classes at Tallahassee Community College.

His unit was called for active duty in January of 2003 and sent to Iraq the following month. Of the war, Robert, a machine-gunner, said resolutely to his dad: "I would rather face them there than here."

Even under extreme pressure, Robert maintained his good humor, as is confirmed by the sweet and teasing correspondence that he shared with his mother, whom he affectionately refers to as "Madda," and his girlfriend, Jenny Walsh. One thing in the following letters may seem cryptic: Robert always included the phrase "just in case" in his closing words to Tammy. It was a running joke between them. They both knew, of course, that he was her only son, but when he signed his letters to her, he would write out his first and last name "just in case" there was another Robert in her life.

On November 12, 2003, Wise, 21, was killed by a bomb that exploded ten feet from the humvee in which he was traveling on a Baghdad street.

Wise was a superhero as a boy, and now his mother tries to be one as she comforts Jenny in Tallahassee.

tell you enough, how much I LOVE YOU! No matter what lays ahead for us, the one thing I know is that we can always do it together. The more I look ahead, the more I realize I can't do it without you. I MISS YOU SOOOOOOOOOOO MUCH! I CAN'T WAIT TO HAVE YOU IN MY ARMS AGAIN!

Well baby, I'm gonna go, so be safe, look after Mom & everybody else, and I'll be home before you know it.

I ♥ U ♡

My Heart & Soul are Forever Yours,

Robert Wise

P.S. This is some Iraq Money (Don't spend it all in one place) There's 2 bills 250 Dinars a piece

Robert Wise

There's no place Like Home (click)
There's no pace like Home (click)
THERE'S NO PLACE LIKE HOME! (click)
Damn, it didn't work again!

Dear Madda,

So far I've been in a sandstorm (twice). I'm working on a third one as I speak (or write). I've also had the pleasure of experiencing a "sand bomb." . . . When the wind is blowing really strong, it fills the tents, but when the wind stops, all the air rushes out of the tent and causes the sand to literally explode into the air, and covers everything in a fine coat of dust. Yeah! Every morning I wake up, and it's like a scene out of the The Mummy. I get to shake dirt out of everything, including my face and hair . . . In case you were wondering, I stink. We call it, "The Scent of the Desert Rose." . . . Anyway, onto more positive news, since Fort Stewart, I've read The Hobbit, Halo, The Lord of the Rings—(The Fellowship of the Ring + The Two Towers . . .)—and Star Trek Eugenics War, Volume II.

Well, I hope everything back at Ft. Living Room is going well.

Always Your Loving Son,
I Miss You & I Love You,
Robert Wise (just in case)

* * * * *

Dear Madda,

Rumor has it that we'll be on a plane home June 22, so keep your fingers crossed. I'm really going to need your help setting up a budget when I get home and making sure I stick to it. I know the only way I'll complete my goals of paying off my car and getting all of that furniture for our (meaning mine + Jenny's) house by the end of the year is by paying attention to what I spend my money on. I'm also going to try and get back into great shape by the end of the year.

I sent off a letter to Jenny about a week back with my ideas on how to set the floor plan in the house. I'm gonna end up buying a couch and a love seat, nice dressers, and other furniture . . . Tell everyone I said "hi," and one day I'll get home.

Your loving son,
Robert Wise (Just in case!)

There's no place like Home (click)
There's no place like Home (click)
THERE'S NO PLACE LIKE HOME! (click)
Damn, it didn't work again!

Tis But a Scratch!

Dear Madda,

What's Up! I hope you feel like me when I call, because it always keeps me smiling for the next week or two. It really brightens my day when we get to chat for a few minutes. Enclosed is a picture & price of the computer I want to buy. It's blue (of course), $989.00, (cyberpowerinc.com) and it's called the Gamer X-treme Lightning Pro. I won't order it until I get home, but it's something to think about.

I'm supposed to get my pictures tonight, so this will go out (I think that's wrong) tomorrow . . . I wanna go home! I'm still trying to find you some fabric, but every time we walk by the stores, they're closed by the time we get back. The last time I weighed my self, I came in at a light 180 pounds. I've lost about 17 pounds since December so hoping to lose about 5 to 10 more pounds, but that would mean going on a healthy diet & constant exercise. The problem with that is that we don't have healthy food, and our shifts are always rotating so it's kinda hard to set up a workout plan. I wish I could buy some furniture over here, but we have no way of getting it home.

I just took a break for a while. I went for a short run about 15 minutes or so, but at 103°, that's a pretty hard workout. I just re-weighed myself, and I'm weighing in at a wopping 169.4 pounds. I guess that's what happens when you hardly eat & sweat all day. Don't worry, I'm not Annorexic, I just don't quite eat like I used to.

Anyways, here are the pictures. I'll explain the others when I get home.

!I love You & I Miss you!

Forever Your Favorite Son (like you had a choice)

Robert Wise (Just in case)

P.S. I found you some fabric!

A decal on the porch door of the family home emphasizes a sentiment Robert held till his death.

Wise was posthumously awarded the Bronze Star, a Purple Heart and the Florida Cross. On November 24, 2003, he was the first Florida National Guard soldier killed in action to be buried in Arlington National Cemetery in Virginia. And at a memorial service for her son in Tallahassee that was attended by more than 1,000 people, Tammy Wise said, "I always knew my son was a great person. But I didn't know everyone else knew it, too. I love you Robert Wise. Just in case."

Spc. Michelle Witmer, Army

She was beloved here, and over there as well.

"Michelle! Michelle!" sang a gleeful chorus of Iraqi children each time she arrived at her Baghdad police station. They knew her well, this singular American soldier. She had reached out to them in a way that was rare.

Michelle "Shelly" Witmer learned compassion at home. The Witmer family of Wisconsin was a tight-knit group of seven—parents Lori and John, children Rachel, Timothy, Charity, Michelle and Mark. Home-schooled during their early years in the Milwaukee suburb of New Berlin, the Witmer kids were best friends as well as kin. Michelle was especially close to her big sister, Rachel, and to her twin, Charity.

At 10, Michelle announced to her sisters that she wanted to be a "hero" when she grew up. After high school, Michelle headed down a path that might allow this, following in her sisters' footsteps by joining the Army National Guard. She had watched as the military had imbued Rachel and Charity with a deepened sense of purpose. This vocation was clearly for her (and it offered a chance to pay for a college education, to boot).

Although she came to regard it as the most difficult thing she'd ever done, Michelle thrived during basic training and graduated with honors. Then it was time for another decision, and the sensitive teen found that having options was trickier than the structured existence of boot camp. Should she enter the Army full-time? Should she finish her education? Ultimately, Shelly enrolled at the University of Wisconsin, Milwaukee, to study broadcast journalism. But in February 2003, before she could begin, she and Rachel both received word that they were being called for active duty with the National Guard and were deployed to Iraq after the fighting began. Nine months later, Charity would be given the same orders.

Even faced with the prospect of deployment, Michelle never dreamed she would wind up with such a dangerous tour of duty. By June 2003, she was working seven-day weeks at a police station in one of Baghdad's toughest areas. (Rachel patrolled the same district with a different platoon.) Michelle's unit was charged with maintaining order amidst chaos, conducting criminal investigations, somehow keeping peace in a place of constant violence. As a "combat lifesaver," Michelle treated everything from concussions to stab wounds. In letters to her family, she tried to remain ever-positive, insisting that she considered her experiences in Iraq "spices" that gave her life "richer flavors." Sometimes, when she was exhausted, her guard fell, and she wrote with intimations of despair.

Even under pressure she remained a selfless friend: One night, when a fellow soldier was feeling depressed, Witmer suddenly leapt to her feet and declared, "Let's go salsa on the roof!" And that, the women did—for what seemed like hours.

Witmer rarely had time off, but nevertheless chose to volunteer at a nearby orphanage (which, in an extraordinary circumstance considering Witmer's situation with her in-country siblings, was named Sisters of Charity). She became a hero to the children, who visited her at the station when she couldn't get to them.

Michelle wrote about all of this—the surreality of Baghdad, the children—in a series of revealing letters to her family. In early April 2004, she was expressing hope that she might be home in a month. But then, on the night of April 9, her convoy drove into an ambush and Michelle Witmer, 20, was fatally wounded.

She had wondered if she might write a book about the war one day. With her death, the letters become her lasting narrative.

Witmers get wet in the late 1980s. Opposite: In New Berlin, the brothers Timothy and Mark stand behind their parents, while Rachel (left) comforts Charity.

4/July/2003

Dear Mom, Dad, Mark, Charity, & Timmy,

I hope you all are doing well. Well I've been in Baghdad for close to a week now and its like nothing I could have ever imagined. We are staying at what was, once a beautiful country club/home that belonged to one of Saddam's close advisors. He was a known terrorist and "the King of spades" in the deck of cards, with all saddams advisors & most wanted. At one time this place must have been spectacular and beautiful but it was bombed pretty badly, and now all thats left is crumbling buildings and remnants of marble floors & staircases, gold class knobs and light fixtures, persian rugs half burned... it truly must have been great. The grounds are bonkers with palm trees and flowers and all the gardens and grass are overgrown but at one time I'm sure they were perfectly manicured and the gardens... Well I can only imagine. It's really more like a ~~~ we don't have electricity. We built makeshift Port-a-pottys (civilian crappers as there referred to by everyone here) hopefully soon we will have running water. It's really heartbreaking to see the poverty right outside the gates where we live and think about how saddam and his crew were living. The children literally swarm you bawling little peddlers were and throwing cry after us saying Misses Misses ...please water please food. & these children usually wander around in filthy clothes and no shoes some of them can't be more than 4 yrs old. It breaks my heart not to be able to give them anything. the police station I work at is in the worst part of Baghdad the area is like

---

(2)

the kind of ghetto, the only thing I can compare it too is maybe like the worst parts of New York or Chicago except with no justice system we are the police and right now the city's in chaos, and it's going to take a long long time to make even a small dent. There are no working stoplights or traffic signs. The traffic is insane. People drive like maniacs. Yesterday morning there was a drive by in front of our station and 2 Iraqi's were killed shot in the head in their car. The station is only sort of like the mexican police stations in movies a filthy little whole in the wall run by crooked cops who are for and don't have much to lose. There are no doors except for the one that leaks in the prisoners two of the people in our holding cell are murders, then there are a bunch of thieves and rockers and a few more who we hold overnight and then release. I work the night shift 7pm to 7am, It's very frightening being in the worst ghetto you can ever imagine at night in the dark, and not only do we have to worry about common criminal gang activity but also the pockets of resistance who support saddam still frequently shoot at our building, and are very much a threat. I hear gunfire all the time its so unnerving. Last night Rachel's station which is a lot nicer than mine got attacked, noone was hurt but it was scary, and they returned fire. I sat and talked to the arabic interpret this for a long time last night. There are two and they both are fluent in English one of them is also fluent in Russian and the other also speaks ?

---

(3)

Chinese. It's amazing. They are teaching me 3 words a day in arabic wow is it difficult! The one of them used to work at an Iraqi Television Studio before the war as a sound tech but we was thrown into ? in order there was an audio problem with one of saddams speeches, they Saddams men beat him and smashed his hands they are pretty much healed but his nuts will be black forever. He was thrown in there for two months, and by prison I mean a tiny cell underground with no windows and about 25 other men. He said that he was on the verge of death, his 5th day without food or water he said he would feel for puddles on the bottom of the cell floor (he couldn't see because it was pitch dark underground) and try to lick up everything he could find, water. Two men had already died from lack of food & water. Then the marines came and broke down the door gave everyone water. They asked me if I could walk home, I told them yes! He said his family was so happy to see him alive. He said he still has dreams about it. This was a educated college grad fluent in many languages who made a mistake on the sound board. Saddams was evil. It's overwhelming to talk first hand to these Iraqis and glimpse the insanity - there were pictures and huge statues of him everywhere.) Most of them are defaced but its so crazy. The culture of Islam is really interesting its hard to get past the men staring at the females in uniform, all the Islamic women wear these black outfits that look similar to a nuns habit. Women aren't seen in public very much, and I always wonder what these people are thinking when they stare at us as

---

We cruise by in the Hummers. Everything we've trained for is coming into play, its a whole different world. I have been up for 18 hours now so I'm not even sure if this letter makes sense anymore... I must sleep now. ? my ? Grammatical errors I'm sure theres at least a hundred. Right now I don't care. Please pray for me this is no cake walk. I love you all so much. I'll try to write again soon.

Love
Michelle Withrow

p.s. I just got promoted so please change that on your site!

---

(1)

Dear mom & Dad,

There is so much to tell you I'm not exactly sure where to begin. Well in the past week I have seen things that I hope & pray I won't forget but somehow their memories will stain my mind forever. I treated a man yesterday after he was pistol whipped to the back of the head in a fight with a group of Iraqis that are wanted for armed robbery he was trying to help the iraqi police catch them when someone came up from behind and hit him very hard on the top of his head with their weapon. He suffered a concussion and their was a lot of blood. I am a combat lifesaver so I treated him, he needed stitches and kept coming in and out conscious the gun was too much for him and he started trying to bang his head against the brick wall of the police station in order to knock himself out. I had no pain killers to give him I told him (after treating the wound as best I could covers my limited supplies) do go to the hospital but he didn't want to go, so I got his sworn statement from him and had to send him off. In the past week I have also seen my first dead body. A group of Iraqi's wheeled a cart in from the street, a man had been shot in the abdomen after trying to steal something about an hour earlier and they put him on the cart and gave him to us to deal with. We deal on a daily basis, with murders, pedophiles, thieves, and every kind of crime you can think of. It's a very dangerous job, I never imagined they would be having us do this kind of work. A grenade was thrown

---

(2)

at our station yesterday but we surprised the guy that was going to throw it and by some miracle he didn't get a chance to pull the pin, and it didn't go off. we had it removed but it was very scary. We took sniper fire twice later on through the evening. yesterday at a different police station, CNN was their to interview some of the people in our company because the 4th platoons station was hit with heavy fire and a terrorist threw 3 grenades at the station - luckily noone was hurt from our company, but 3 civilians and 2 Iraqi policemen were killed. You know the twin towers, the huge mess of rubble, thats how virtually every building in the city looks. We have it so good these people are ruthless, they have been murdered by years of seeing their loved ones killed, dealing with war, terror, and everything you can imagine. I work the night shift and the days sort of run into each other I don't know what day of the week it is most of the time. We have one of the most dangerous jobs in Baghdad and even though I will keep my cool when I'm working the stress does take a toll and I'll get back to my cot and cry for a little while and then fall asleep almost immediately. It is hard to be a woman in this environment the Iraqi police are polite but they certainly don't think we belong there. I work with only one other female and I really miss Rachel or the other female I work with has some kind of social disorder she sort of reminds me of Howard and is almost impossible to talk with. She really shouldn't even ?

---

(3)

be on this deployment but she does most of the paperwork. I miss you all so much! I'm earning every penny of what I'm making thats for sure! This is the most real police work you could do, people come in bleeding after gunfights, beat or with stab wounds, or with information about terrorists, or asking for protection from the terrorists they used to work with, just everything. We have to interview, interrogate, take statements, collect evidence, it is a lot of paperwork! I know one thing for sure I wouldn't want to be a cop in the civilian world. Please pray for me (Please send me letters I need to the encouragement!) I love you all. I gotta get some sleep now.

♡ Shelly
(Spc. Withrow)

Dear Mom & Dad,

There is so much to tell you I'm not exactly sure where to begin. Well in the past week I have seen things that I hope very much to forget, but somehow their memories will stain my mind forever. I treated a man yesterday after he was pistol whipped to the back of the head in a fight with a group of Iraqis that are wanted for armed robbery. He was trying to help the Iraqi police catch them when someone came up from behind and hit him very hard on the top of his head with their weapon. He suffered a concussion and their was a lot of blood. I am a combat Lifesaver so I treated him. He needed stitches and kept coming in and out of conscienceness (sp). The pain was too much for him and he started trying to bang his head agains the brick wall at the police station in order to knock himself out (it took 3 men to restrain him). I had no painkillers to give him. I told him (after treating the wound as best I could given my limited supplies) to go to the hosipital but he didn't want to go, so I got his sworn statement from him and had to send him off.

In the past week I have also seen my first dead body. A group of Iraqis wheeled a cart in from the street. A man had been shot in the abdomen after trying to steal something about an hour earlier, and they put him on the cart and gave him to us to deal with. We deal on a daily basis, with murders, pedafiles, thieves, and every kind of crime you can think of. It's a very dangerous job. I never imagined they would be having us do this kind of work.

A grenade was thrown at our station yesterday but we surprised the guy that was going to throw it and by some miracle he didn't get a chance to pull the pin, and it didn't go off. We had it removed but it was very scary. We took sniper fire twice later on through the evening. Yesterday . . . a terrorist threw 3 grenades at [another] station—luckily noone was hurt from our company, but 3 civilians and 2 Iraqi policemen were killed. You know the twin towers, the huge mess of rubble, thats how virtually every building in the city looks. We have it <u>so</u> good in America. These people are ruthless. They have been hardened by years of seeing their loved ones killed, dealing with war, terror, and everything you can imagine.

It is hard to be a woman [here]. The Iraqi police are polite but they certainly don't think we belong there. I work with only one other female and I really miss Rachel.

I miss you all so much . . . <u>Please</u> pray for me! Please send me letters. [I] need the encouragement! I love you all. I gotta get some sleep now.
   ❤
Shelly
(Spc. Witmer)

Dear Daddy,

Happy Father's Day!

I love you so much and you can't imagine how often I think of you. I hope you have lots of fun today and that the weather is lovely.

We had a briefing telling us to prepare ourselves as best as possible for what lies ahead. Things like children running out in front of the vehicles to try and get them to stop. We have to prepare ourselves to hit people because stopping is not an option. I guess every convoy that's gone up north so far has taken fire or been ambushed. The question of whether we will or not is not even really a question, more like a guess as to when.

These things, as you can imagine, are a lot to take in.

I'm doing my best. I've been a little depressed lately but I'm trying to keep my chin up. I really miss home. Tomorrow will be exactly 3 months since I got deployed. Wow—time does not fly. Geez, this letter wasn't supposed to be so down. Sorry.

Back to the point: Happy Father's Day! I love you and miss you sooo much.

Love,
Shelly

Rachel, Charity, Lori and Michelle share a proud
moment before the daughters' deployment. Right:
Her lasting legacy in Iraq is to the children.
On the following page: Michelle's helmet and medals.

Specialist Witmer's funeral was held on April 14, 2004, in Brookfield, Wis. She
was posthumously awarded a Purple Heart, the Bronze Star and the National
Defense Service Medal. Rachel and Charity, who were given the option of reas-
signment to non-combat positions, chose not to return to Iraq.

And the memorial fund established in Michelle Witmer's honor will, fittingly,
benefit those children at the Sisters of Charity Orphanage in Baghdad—perhaps
the very ones who used to sing out her name.